Why Do You Do That?

of related interest

Tics and Tourette Syndrome
A Handbook for Parents and Professionals
Uttom Chowdhury
Foreword by Isobel Heyman
ISBN 1 84310 203 X

Disorganized Children
A Guide for Parents and Professionals
Edited by Samuel M. Stein and Uttom Chowdhury
ISBN 1 84310 148 3

Kids in the Syndrome Mix of ADHD, LD, Asperger's, Tourette's, Bipolar, and More!
The one stop guide for parents, teachers, and other professionals
Martin L. Kutscher
With contributions from Tony Attwood and Robert R. Wolff
ISBN 1 84310 810 0 hb
ISBN 1 84310 811 9 pb

Genius!
Nurturing the Spirit of the Wild, Odd, and Oppositional Child – Revised Edition
George T. Lynn with Joanne Barrie Lynn
ISBN 1 84310 820 8

Asperger's Syndrome
A Guide for Parents and Professionals
Tony Attwood
Foreword by Lorna Wing
ISBN 1 85302 577 1

Why Do You Do That?

A Book about Tourette Syndrome for Children and Young People

Uttom Chowdhury and Mary Robertson

Illustrated by Liz Whallett

Foreword by Tim Howard

Jessica Kingsley Publishers
London and Philadelphia

First published in 2006
by Jessica Kingsley Publishers
116 Pentonville Road
London N1 9JB, UK
and
400 Market Street, Suite 400
Philadelphia, PA 19106, USA

www.jkp.com

Library of Congress Cataloging in Publication Data
A CIP catalog record for this book is available from the Library of Congress

British Library Cataloguing in Publication Data
A CIP catalogue record for this book is available from the British Library

ISBN-13: 978 1 84310 395 0
ISBN-10: 1 84310 395 8

Printed and bound in Great Britain by
Athenaeum Press, Gateshead, Tyne and Wear

Contents

Foreword

Why Do You Do That? is an outstanding resource both for those, like me, who have Tourette Syndrome, and for all those family members, friends and associates of those with Tourette Syndrome who wish to know more about the condition. I have always said that Tourette Syndrome is a speed bump, not a road block, on the road to achieving what you want to achieve in life. Certainly, a large part of getting over that speed bump is understanding. If you have Tourette Syndrome, you need to understand what it means, and what it does not mean, and become comfortable with who you are. And those around those with Tourette Syndrome would do well to understand the condition better so that they might help and not hinder. This book is of great use on both fronts.

Tim Howard, Goalkeeper,
Manchester United and USA

Acknowledgements

Ivan Astin

Lana-Emerald Astin

Rachel Bermingham

Jeannette Berrill

Amber Carroll

Rebecca Chilvers

Sam Cosham

Kaye Dann

Kevin Dann

Jacqui Davies

Rosemary Dixon

Hannah Eisman-Renyard

Stephanie Gee

Tarun Goel

Sheena Grigor

Sigrun Gunnarsdottir

Anneke Haddad

Deborah Harwood

Zoe Harwood

Karen Hjartardottir

Zak Hollis

Noreen Kingston

Maria Letizia

Sue Levi Pearl

John Ludgate

Jill Metcalfe

Natalie Jane Shears

Susan Morley

Yoshiko Nomura

Ling Po

Alison Reeve

Renato Rizzo

Graham Rugg

Perminder Sachdev

Daniel Said

Joshua Skaug

Samuel Stein

Jeremy Stern

Katya Strassburger

Max Strassburger

Joanne Todd

Sally Todd

Lance Turtle

Judit Ungar

Huei-Shyong Wang

Rosie Wartdecker

Chi-Wee

Ken Yoshizawa

Tourette Syndrome (Australia) Association

Tourette Syndrome (Iceland) Association

Tourette Syndrome (Japan) Association

Tourette Syndrome (Taiwan) Association

Tourette Syndrome (UK) Association

Tourette Syndrome (USA) Association

Chapter 1

What is Tourette Syndrome?

What is Tourette Syndrome?

Tourette Syndrome is when a person has movements and noises which they can't really control and they have had them for at least one year. Doctors give movements a medical name called 'motor tics' and noises a medical name called 'vocal or phonic tics'.

A lot of people with Tourette Syndrome call it TS. Most doctors and other people who help those with Tourette Syndrome also call it TS.

What is a tic?

A tic is a muscle movement or noise which the person cannot help doing. The tics are fast and happen again and again and they are not done on purpose. The tics are unnecessary because they do not fulfil a function or do anything that is important. For example, a movement tic or action may be a blink when the person has nothing in his or her eye. A noise tic may be a sniff when someone has no snot in their nose, or a cough when the person does not have a cold.

Tics are simple movements which repeat over and over again. They can also be actions which may look as though they are being done on purpose. This can look as if the person is pulling a funny face, when there is nobody else there to see him or her. The noises can be normal noises like coughing, or strange noises like barking like a dog. Sometimes the movements and noises can look like normal behaviour like smiling often, when he or she does not mean to smile. Sometimes the tics can look like very unusual behaviour. For example, when somebody is walking along a road, they may suddenly turn round and skip for no reason at all.

Where does the name Tourette Syndrome come from?

There was a famous doctor who had a very long name: Georges Albert Edouard Brutus Gilles de la Tourette. He was born about 150 years ago in 1857 and lived in the capital of France, Paris. He worked at a well-known hospital called the Salpêtrière which was, and still is, one of the most famous hospitals in the world. He wrote in a medical book the stories of nine patients who had many tics and other symptoms. He was the first person to suggest that this group of problems found together in one person could form one separate condition. Doctor Gilles de la Tourette also used to study hysteria, dizziness and hypnosis – a kind of sleep therapy. He also had an interesting project in which he used footprints to diagnose nervous disease. He died in 1904 in Switzerland. But, thanks to him, his story and that of so many people lives on.

What are the signs of TS?

The most important signs, and the ones which have to be present in order for doctors to call it TS, are both the movements and the noises. As we have said before, these tics must have been there for at least a year. Many young people call them habits.

Tics can be simple or complicated. Simple motor tics are fast and meaningless and include eye blinking, making faces and shoulder shrugging. Complicated tics are usually slower and may look as though they may have been done on purpose. The person may hop, or even kiss others (without a cuddle!) or kiss themselves (when they don't want to) or touch things (such as hot cookers – ouch!) or people who may even be strangers, and this can be very embarrassing. The person may also copy movements, tics or normal smiles of other people which has a name: echopraxia. This makes other people think that the person is 'taking the mickey' and this can also get them into trouble. A few young people make rude signs, like the 'V' sign or the 'third finger' sign, which doctors give a strange name called 'copropraxia'. Obviously doing the 'V' sign in public gets you into trouble. And if the young person does not have TS, it should get them into trouble!

Simple vocal tics include coughing, barking and clearing the throat. Some people have complex vocal tics such as repeating certain words or sayings such as 'oh boy' or 'all right' or repeating a sentence until it sounds 'just right'. Other complex vocal tics include changes in speech, such as changes in the rhythm, the tone or the speed of the voice.

A few people with TS say rude words which are also known as 'swearing tics'. The person may say 'f**k off' but not mean it. The person often tries to hide the 'F-word tic' by covering it up and doing something like a cough so that the swear word is not obvious. Doctors give this sign a medical name called 'coprolalia'.

It is usual for tics to come and go. They change in how severe they are and how often they occur. These changes occur during each day as well as between days. This is often referred to as 'waxing and waning'.

Many people get a funny feeling before the tic. This can be in the area of the tic (such as in the area of the nose before a sniff) or more general. We have seen patients who feel funny all over their chest and tummy before a tic. When the person has their tic, this funny feeling goes away. Doctors call these feelings 'premonitory sensations'. Lots of our young TS patients have told us that this funny feeling is very similar to the feeling you get just before a sneeze. You feel the sneeze coming, you have to do it and then you feel better afterwards.

Tics often get stronger and are most obvious at around the ages of 10 to 12 years. The tics often reduce and in some people disappear by the age of 18 years. For many people the tics are stable by the time they are grown-ups. Very recently doctors have written that although people may still have tics when they are older, they cope with them quite well.

The person with TS often has a number of different motor and vocal tics, but head and neck tics are by far the commonest. The head tics are nodding, and flicking the hair out of the eyes. Sadly we have had young patients who have been teased and called 'Noddy' and they have been very upset by this. We are sure that we or you would be upset by this also. We have had other patients who have flicked their hair out of their eyes so much that their mum and dad have taken them to the hairdresser or barber to have their fringes cut. But as this is a tic (and not really getting the hair out of the eyes), it continues even after the hair has been cut. For other young people who blink a lot, their mums and dads have taken them to opticians. Of course, as there is nothing really wrong with their eyes, the opticians tell them that there is nothing wrong with them or their eyes. Only half of this is true. There is probably nothing wrong with their eyes but they may have tics or TS. Other mums and dads take their children who sniff or cough to doctors who deal with people's throats and noses. In England we call them ENT doctors, but in America they are called otolaryngologists. Again these doctors say after they have examined the child, there is nothing wrong as there is nothing wrong with their throat or nose. Again they have tics and maybe TS.

The swearing tic is very uncommon in children and only occurs in fewer than one third of grown-ups who attend special clinics. Some doctors who do not know much about TS still think that the swearing tic has to be present for them to diagnose TS. This is not true. The newspapers and television often show the swearing tic as part of TS. It is understandable because if there was a story about a boy who only blinked his eyes, nobody would read it. This may be because blinking is normal and a blinking tic is quite common. However, swearing is not allowed in many homes and at school, and therefore writing about swearing and showing it on television is said to be interesting and funny.

People with TS can stop their tics for a short period of time only by concentrating a lot. In school this sometimes confuses teachers. We can understand this, because if the child can stop his or her tics, then many people will say that the child is putting his or her tics on, on purpose. We know that this is not true but some children still get into trouble for their tics at school.

Many children find that when they are concentrating or thinking hard on a particular task, such as playing a computer game or game boy, their tics are not so obvious. The tics may also become more obvious during times when children are relaxed after a stressful period such as when they are returning home from school or having sat an exam.

In the past it was thought that tics disappear during sleep but recent studies have shown that tics are present during sleep. Quite a lot of children find that the tics actually stop them from going to sleep easily. Lots of brothers and sisters find this quite annoying. If their brother or sister makes noises in the night, it can wake them up. When they grow up, get married and sleep in the same bed as someone, the tics or jerks can wake up the person they love.

Swearing and the F-word tic

The swearing seen in TS is known as *coprolalia*. This is the use of rude or unacceptable words or phrases. This is very different to the 'social' swearing seen at school or in some homes. If we are cross (and we know we shouldn't be), we sometimes tell our mates to f**k off. Usually we only do this when adults or teachers are not around, so we do not get into trouble. We swear deliberately and mean it. When a boy with TS swears, he does not mean it, it usually happens when people least expect it (not during a fight or when he is angry) and he has little or no control over it. In other words he cannot help it. He often tries to cover it up by coughing and covering his mouth. He feels embarrassed and upset by it and is apologetic or says 'sorry' afterwards.

When does TS begin?

The start of tics can be in children as young as 3 years old. Most children start their tics between 5 and 7 years. If a person is going to get a diagnosis of TS, the tics must start by the age of 21 years. Another way of looking at this is that TS is a condition which starts in children and young people. Boys get TS more than girls. The first tics are often blinking, head and neck twitching or throat clearing.

What is it like for someone who has TS?

Our patients in the clinic often describe what doctors call a 'premonitory' feeling or sensation before the tics which are separate from the actual tic itself. The feeling is briefly relieved or feels better after the tic has happened. Examples of these sensations include a burning feeling in the eye before an eye blink, itching before a movement of the shoulders, tension in the neck that is relieved by stretching the neck or a funny feeling in the nose which is like the feeling before a sneeze and then which feels better after the sneeze.

We had a patient who had a funny feeling in her neck. It was so powerful that the only way she could cope was to punch herself in the neck. This upset the child and also her family as it looked sore and in fact must have been sore. We know because she told us that she found it very upsetting. It made her cry. In fact we were also upset.

Some myths about Tourette Syndrome

He/she swears because he/she has TS
Only a few children with TS use swear words – most do not. If they do, it is usually out of context (in other words, not meant), said quickly and the child is often very apologetic afterwards.

He/she is making those noises on purpose
This is not true. Children may be able to control tics for a few seconds but sooner or later they have to 'release' their tic.

He/she has a mental illness
Tourette Syndrome is not a mental illness – it is a medical disorder that may have psychological symptoms. Psychiatrists are often involved since they have expertise with dealing with TS and the related behavioural and emotional problems.

He/she will never get a job or have a special relationship
Many people with TS go on to lead normal, rich lives and have fulfilling healthy relationships. Examples of famous people who are thought to have TS include Tim Howard (Manchester United Football Team Goalkeeper), Dr Samuel Johnson, who wrote the English dictionary, and Jim Eisenreich, a famous major league baseball player in America (see Chapter 8).

Wynken, Blynken and Nod

Wynken and Blynken are your little eyes
And Nod is your little bobbing head
Most people keep them still – no surprise
But for Touretters, that's only while asleep in bed.

I have many tics, and some are bad
When my TS hurts, it makes me so sad,
I blink, wink, spit, or shout out loud,
It makes me stand out in a big crowd.

Others call them tics, I call it my habit,
Some people say my nose is like a rabbit,
I sniff, clear my throat, and also cough,
I copy others too: but enough is enough!

Mary M. Robertson
With apologies to Eugene Field

Chapter 2

What have research doctors found out about Tourette Syndrome?

Introduction

We have met hundreds of young people with TS who have been our patients in the clinic. Nearly all our patients, even those who are quite young children, ask us many questions about their condition, TS. These questions are about the cause of TS, how common it is, how TS is treated, and what the future is of a young person with TS.

Where does TS come from and can I catch TS?

No, you cannot catch TS like you catch the flu, measles, mumps or chicken pox. You are born with it. Mostly TS and tics run in families. This is like having height, dark hair or a certain eye colour which is passed down from parent to child. Doctors call this inheriting a condition and the science is known as genetics. A chromosome is a structure which is found in all living cells and it is made up of threads of DNA and protein. The chromosome carries the genes which are the basic unit of heredity or cause us to inherit various conditions.

This often means that if Dad has tics, his son may have tics or TS. We will talk about it later, but if a girl child inherits the condition she may show other behaviours which are common in TS. It is important to understand that this does not mean that it is Dad's fault if a child inherits TS. It is like inheriting being tall. Some children are tall and some children are short.

One of the problems with what we call the genetics of TS (that is how it runs in families) is that not all people carrying the gene for TS will show the symptoms of TS. This person will be called a 'carrier'. Also some research doctors have shown that boys get tics and TS, whereas girls may get obsessional behaviours which will be discussed in Chapter 3.

Many studies are being done in the world on the cause of TS, and lots of doctors work together on the genetics of TS. In fact there is a big world-wide group of doctors from America, Canada, England, Holland and South Africa who have been working together as a team for many years, looking for the genes. They have published lots of medical papers or stories about this. This group of doctors has been given a lot of money by an important committee to study this. This is exciting, as this committee also gives money to study other conditions such as depression or trauma. Therefore we are so glad that they think that TS is important enough to give money to do research on it.

Science has advanced a lot in the last ten years. Many years ago it was thought that the genetics of TS was simple and that if a Dad had TS, his son would also inherit TS. Now, however, it seems that the genetics are more complex and probably no one gene is responsible for TS. There is no blood test at present for diagnosing TS. Some doctors do take blood so that tests can be done to rule out any other conditions which could be confused with TS. As we have said already, some boys with the gene may have tics or TS, girls may have obsessional behaviours and others may not have any problems or show any symptoms.

It has been shown that in some cases when mums have difficulties in pregnancy such as feeling sick or vomiting a lot and take medications for this vomiting, and birth difficulties such as the cord being around the neck of the baby, the baby having 'yellow jaundice', the baby being born too young or too small, the baby being delivered by operation (called Caesarean section), the baby being born by an instrumental or forceps delivery, or after a very long labour, the child may be more likely to get TS than a child born to the same mother with a completely normal pregnancy and birth. Obviously once again if the child's mum does have a difficult birth and the child does get TS, it is not Mum's fault. Actually it is not the doctor's fault either, it is just one of those things. When you get older you will realise that many things in life are in fact 'just one of those things' that we can't do anything about. They just happen. The weather is sometimes bad when we are on holiday or vacation and there is just nothing we can do about it – 'That's Life!'

PANDAS

No, we are not talking about panda bears, which you may have seen in the zoo. Recently, some doctors have found that some infections work in more complex or difficult ways than it was once thought, and may also give a child a greater risk or chance of having tics or even TS. Because this subject is complex, even for us, we are only going to give an outline that we hope you will understand. The infections we are talking about include a special type of germ called Streptococcus, which is normally found on the skin and in the guts of people. Different types of Streptococcus can cause a variety of infections in human beings including sore throats. Most of you will have had a sore throat in your lives and many have had Streptococcal infections – but you may not have known that at the time. It has been suggested that if a person inherits the gene or genes for TS, and they then catch a Steptococcal germ and infection, the way they react to the infection may be different to people who just get ordinary sore throats. These people may get tics and other signs of TS and the behaviours which can be seen in TS. Most of us will just get a sore throat. We will discuss these other behaviours later. What is important to understand is that this type of infection is not normally treated by taking an antibiotic which is a pill or tablet used for destroying disease-causing bugs. This is interesting, but in fact more studies need to be done before this idea is certain.

How many other young people have TS?

The first person with TS was described by Doctor Itard a long time ago in 1825. Doctor Gilles de la Tourette then decribed nine people with TS in 1885. Then several doctors saw people with TS, and wrote up their stories in medical books or 'journals'. For many years TS was thought to be very uncommon. In fact, right up until the mid 1990s, TS was thought to affect only between five and ten people per 100,000. That is very few and TS was thought to be very uncommon. Then, many doctors who have a special interest in TS started studying how common TS may be. Since the year 2000, there have been studies coming from America, England, Sweden, Italy, China and Taiwan in the Far East, all showing that TS is more common than was once thought. All these studies have been done on schoolchildren and so lots of children like those reading this book may have taken part in the studies. Of course in studies like this, no child and no school is named.

Now it is thought that about 0.4 per cent to 1.76 per cent of children between the ages of 5 and 18 may have TS. It is easier to have one figure or number to think of and thus we suggest we use the number of 1 per cent as it is about half way between 0.4 per cent and 1.76 per cent. This means that as many as one in a hundred children may have TS. This may mean that as many as 90,000 young people in the United Kingdom have TS. Most of these youngsters however will have mild signs and will not have been diagnosed in a doctor's clinic.

About one in a hundred young people between the ages of 5 and 18 years may have mild TS. This could be as many as 90,000 in the UK.

In some children who have learning difficulties, special educational needs or a disorder of development called autism, even more may have TS and numbers over 5 per cent have been suggested. In other words, in these people TS is quite common.

In most of these young people with TS whom doctors find in the community or special schools, the TS is most likely to be mild and may not have been diagnosed by anybody before the research doctor did.

Am I the only person in the world with TS?

You may think and feel like you are the only child with TS. As we have already said, TS is now thought to be quite common. TS is in fact found in people all over the world and has been described or is recognised in nearly all of the countries you could name, starting from A and going all the way through to Z. So, you will see that in the medical books and papers, people with TS have been described from well-known countries such as Argentina, Australia, Austria, Belgium, Brazil, Bulgaria, Canada, Chile, China, Columbia, Croatia, Cyprus, Denmark, Ecuador, Finland, France, Germany, Great Britain, Greece, Holland, Hungary, Iceland, India, Iraq, Ireland, Israel, Italy, Japan, Korea, Lithuania, Luxembourg, New Zealand, Norway, Pakistan, Paraguay, Peru, Poland, Russia, South Africa, Spain, Sweden, Switzerland, Taiwan, Thailand, Turkey, United Arab Emirates, United States of America and Zimbabwe – in other words, loads of countries!

It is important to know that the signs of TS are almost identical in every country and culture in the world. The motor tics look the same in every country and the noises such as coughing, throat clearing and sniffing sound the same even though the people with TS may speak different languages. The swear-word tics are similar in every language. Sometimes, the bad word is not necessarily a swear word, but a word that is not acceptable in a culture, such as a bad word about God, of whatever religion (this is known as blasphemy).

In our opinion, the fact that TS is similar in every country really shows that TS is to do with our bodies and brains being slightly different and that it is nothing really to do with our culture.

Will I always have TS?

Not necessarily. The best way to describe how TS can last all of a person's life is to tell you about the first person who was ever described with TS. This was a French noble-woman, the Marquise de Dampierre. She was first written about by Dr Itard in 1825 when she was a young woman. Unfortunately she had many tics and noises, and also had rude and bad language. Because she came from an important family, her rude language was even more unacceptable than it may have been if she had come from an ordinary family. She was forced therefore to live alone in a tower or turret. Funnily enough many people think this is where TS got its name from. You, of course, already know that it came from Dr Georges Gilles de la Tourette. However, it is important to know that she had TS until she died as a very old woman.

It is because of the Marquise and many other adult people that, in the past, most doctors thought that TS began in childhood and stayed with the person forever. It is our experience, and doctors have also written in medical books, that in many young people the signs of TS and the problems that go with them reach a peak that is greatest at about the age of 10 to 12 and then decrease with age. By the age of 18 many people have lost a lot of their tics. In addition, many of the difficulties associated with tics also often disappear. In other words, the Marquise's story is an uncommon outcome.

Of course TS continues to be a problem for some adults with TS, but for some of them TS becomes part of them. Again, some of our grown-up patients with TS have lived with it for so long that it becomes a 'friend' for them. By making their TS a 'friend', this is the way they cope with something they have to live with. For example, we had one patient who called it his 'G and T' (this is also a nice drink that grown-ups have called Gin and Tonic). On the other hand, we understand, however, that for some people TS will never be a friend, either if they have got it, or their brother or sister has got it.

Have there been any studies of the brain in TS?

Many years ago the only way to see what the brain looked like in any condition or disease that affected human beings was to either take a blood sample or, sadly, to examine the person after they had died. Doctors call this examination a 'post mortem' or 'PM' which just means an examination after death. There have been only a few PM studies of people with TS and that is because people do not die of TS.

So the only PM studies in TS have been on people who have died of other causes. Even then, there are few of these people available for examination. It is amazing that even though these examinations and studies were written about so long ago, some of these studies have found very small problems in the part of the brain known as the basal ganglia. The basal ganglia is the part of the brain that is involved with our movements. Two of the biochemicals that go in the nerves between the cells in the basal ganglia and other parts of the brain are called dopamine and serotonin. All this is very complicated.

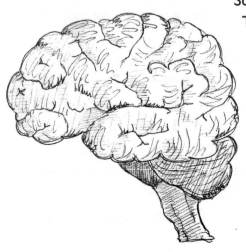

Science today has come a long way. There are machines that can take very fancy and detailed pictures of the brain while the person is awake. The person feels no pain during these special investigations and the only real problems people have had are they feel it is too noisy or the space in the machine is too small.

The machines looking at the brain are called scans. Some machines show the structure of the brain while others show the function of the brain. Let's put it another way: if you take a picture of the nose, you see its structure; that is, its size and shape. The function of the nose is breathing.

The names of the various scans can be seen in the box on the next page.

A particular part of the basal ganglia is a structure called the caudate nucleus. In studies done by doctors it has been shown that this structure is smaller in both children and adults with TS when compared to the caudate nucleus of healthy children and adults, who volunteer to take part in these studies.

Some scans are able to show the functions of the brain and the research doctors can either see the activity levels of sugar (glucose) or the chemicals dopamine and serotonin in the various parts of the brain. Almost all of you, or your brothers and sisters, will know somebody who has had an X-ray when they fell and broke their arm. The X-ray has been around and used for a long time by doctors and is very good for showing up signs such as broken bones. It is not very helpful in TS unless the doctor thinks that the young person may have another medical problem.

This is the same for CT scans. The technical name for this is computerised tomography. It is really a very sophisticated X-ray but can also show parts or structures of the brain as well as the skull bones. The medical name for the MRI is Magnetic Resonance Imaging scan and this uses magnetic waves rather than X-rays. It is very sensitive and can in fact show very small parts or structures of the brain. The brain is made up of white and grey matter and the MRI can actually show differences between the two of them on the scan. Many people, usually adults, have had MRIs to help diagnose other conditions because they are useful in picking up problems in what we doctors call 'soft tissues'.

Very few people with TS nowadays have MRI scans because those MRIs that have been done in the past show that they are not really useful in individual patients and only really show very small differences between groups of patients and a group of healthy people (volunteers) without such a condition as TS.

However, individual patients with TS may need an MRI scan if the doctor is not sure of the diagnosis or suspects that there may be other problems.

The last three types of imaging machines are even more grand and sophisticated and are usually only found in specialist hospitals and centres and usually only used in research. Of course there may be times where a person has one of these tests for a very specific reason, but it does need specially trained doctors and scientists to understand the pictures seen on the imaging screens.

Imaging machines of the brain

X-ray	This can show skull and hardened bits of the brain known as calcification.
CT scan	This shows the insides of the brain better than the X-ray.
MRI	This shows the structure of the brain including white and grey matter
fMRI; PET; SPECT	These three methods are very fancy and are able to show the function of the brain. They are nearly always used for research and hardly ever in an individual patient.

Hospital fever

We must go down to the doctor again, to the hospital tall and high
And all we ask is a specialist, and research to steer us by.
The docs take blood, do EEGs and also scans of the brain
And we see the docs for our results – sadly, again and again.

What causes TS and how much do we people all know?
Doctors have done lots of research, but still have a way to go
We have pictures of the brain, which show the blood flow
And whether the energy and sugar – is high or low.

These fancy brain tests are called SPECT, CT, and MRI
All fancy expensive machines, which our docs use as their eye
To see the brain and its bits, and also how it really works
And what causes our tics and noises, and also our quirks.

The chemicals dopamine and serotonin may have gong wrong
Don't worry – they'll find the cause and cure before long
And then many of the tics and our irritating oddities will go
And they may also find the 'bad' genes – you never know.

Mary M. Robertson
With apologies to John Masefield

Chapter 3

Are there any other problems associated with Tourette Syndrome?

Occasionally other problems can occur with people who have TS. Some people will develop some symptoms, others may not. We think it is worth knowing a little bit about the problems just in case they do occur. If they occur then it may be possible to get help from the doctors or in the classroom.

What is obsessive compulsive disorder?

Many adults and young people have thoughts or ideas that come into their mind even when they do not want them. These thoughts are called obsessions. These thoughts can be silly, do not make sense or are unpleasant. Many people find that they have a need to do certain things such as touching the door-frame over and over again even when they really do not want to do it. This is called a compulsion.

Obsessive compulsive disorder (OCD) is a condition which includes these unwanted thoughts or images (obsessions) and unwanted repetitive acts and rituals (compulsions). Many people have OCD symptoms and many are reluctant to seek help or share their concerns for fear of being ridiculed.

Common obsessions include scary thoughts about germs, thinking that you cannot throw things away (for example newspapers), aggressive images or preoccupation with one's body. The thoughts are usually recognised as irrational and silly. Compulsions include excessive washing, checking, counting and repeating things.

Common obsessions and compulsions	
Obsessions	*Compulsions*
Contamination	Washing
Aggressive	Checking
Sexual	Repeating
Hoarding (not throwing things away)	Need for reassurance
Magical thoughts	Counting
Somatic (physical symptoms)	Ordering
Religious	Arranging
	Hoarding (not throwing things away)

What causes OCD?

Research suggests that OCD is caused by an imbalance of chemicals in the brain. The main chemical is called serotonin. This is a chemical that is found in every brain and is important for regulation of mood. Some children with TS may also have associated OCD or it may be found within family members.

What is the treatment?

There are two main treatments: cognitive behavioural therapy and medication.

Cognitive behavioural therapy

This is a talking treatment that tries to change the way a person feels by altering how they think and how they see and understand their world. The aim of the treatment is to teach the patient how to be in control of his or her problems. It involves tackling the problems a little at a time until the patient has learnt that he or she can overcome small problems. Once this is done, he or she can then move on to the next bigger problem. It is usually carried out by an experienced therapist, usually a psychologist. Often family members can help by working with the therapist and patient to manage the obsessions and rituals.

Medication

Medicines which increase the amount of serotonin in the brain are helpful. These include fluoxetine, sertraline and clomipramine. These medicines can only be prescribed by a medical doctor and the patient will need regular follow-up if on medication.

What is attention deficit hyperactivity disorder?

Attention deficit hyperactivity disorder, or ADHD as it is better known, is a condition which causes young people to have problems with concentration, makes the young person fidgety and restless and often causes problems with waiting in turn. These symptoms are common in many children, but when extreme they can cause a tremendous amount of problems in the individual child. It can also be extremely tiring for the whole family if someone has ADHD.

Symptoms of ADHD

Inattention
Careless with detail
Fails to pay and keep attention
Appears not to listen
Does not finish instructed task
Loses things
Easily distracted
Seems forgetful

Hyperactivity/Impulsivity
Fidgets
Leaves seat when should be seated
Runs/climbs excessively and inappropriately
Noisy in play
Blurts out answers before question completed
Fails to wait turn or to wait in a queue
Interrupts others' conversation or games
Talks excessively

Other associated features include aggressive and naughty behaviour and problems with making and keeping friends. Their impulsivity and failure to think through actions may lead to rule-breaking behaviour. Such children may be easily influenced by others and may well be noticed more than others in class.

ADHD occurs in a large number of children with TS. It may be that it is the ADHD difficulties which cause the child to have difficulties. Many families of children with TS find that they can cope with the tics but it is the ADHD symptoms which cause the most distress for the child and his or her family.

What causes ADHD?

No one knows for certain. Some researchers think it is to do with the front bit of the brain called the frontal lobe. It may also be due to a deficiency in a chemical called dopamine. The disorder does appear to run in families and tends to be more common in boys than girls.

What is the treatment?

The most effective treatment at present is stimulant medication called methylphenidate, of which one type is known as Ritalin. This works by making the person more alert and helps concentration. Occasionally the stimulant medicines can give bad side-effects such as making tics worse. If this happens then the patient and family should consult their doctor. Practical and effective ways of helping the child include lots of boundaries, structure and help with organisation. Parents can often get help from therapists about the best way of managing a person with ADHD. Schools can also be helpful by providing more support, and helping with homework (see Chapter 5).

What is depression?

A lot of young people feel sad and depressed if they have or are experiencing something upsetting or stressful. Usually this only lasts for a short while. If the sadness continues, and it starts to cause problems with life at home or school, then this may be what doctors call clinical depression. The main features are: being unhappy and miserable, having no sense of enjoyment in usual hobbies or interests, difficulty concentrating, becoming withdrawn, becoming more self-critical and blaming oneself, tiredness and no energy, feeling hopeless and occasionally having thoughts of self-harm. Children with TS have been shown to have problems with depression. It is not clear whether the depression is as a result of the tic disorder, or due to other associated factors such as being bullied. Treatment for clinical depression may include counselling, cognitive therapy, and tablets called antidepressants.

What is bipolar affective disorder (BPD)?

BPD is a disorder which causes people to have extreme changes of mood. This may mean that they have times when they are extremely depressed and low and at other times they may be unusually happy and excitable. Many of us have these symptoms, but in BPD the mood swings are extreme and much more than we normally see in others. It is very rare before teenage years and can be very difficult to detect since many teenagers have these symptoms as a healthy part of growing up.

What causes BPD?

No one really knows. We do know that BPD tends to run in families. Sometimes stress can bring about an episode.

Signs of bipolar affective disorder
Depression – low mood
Irritability
Change in appetite
Loss of interest
Withdrawal from social life
Unusually happy
Giggly
Excitable
Reckless behaviour – spending lots of money without concern,
    taking risks
Poor sleep

What is the treatment?

Rest is really important. If it is an isolated episode, then it may settle. Sometimes medicines such as antidepressants may help or other medicines known as antipsychotics.

Mood stabilising medicines such as lithium may need to be prescribed. Doctors need to review and keep a constant check on young people with this problem.

What is anxiety?

Anxiety related conditions such as generalised anxiety disorder, panic attacks and phobias are often seen in children and adults with TS. The symptoms usually involve excessive worrying and fear about something. Physical symptoms include breathlessness, palpitations, dry mouth and stomach pains. Treatment is a form of talking therapy called cognitive behavioural therapy (see obsessive compulsive disorder above).

What is oppositional behaviour?

This involves persistent behaviour by the person, which includes frequent arguments with adults, with them often losing their temper, deliberately annoying others, actively refusing to comply with adults' requests, being easily annoyed by others and being spiteful and vindictive on a regular basis. A collection of these symptoms make up the condition known as oppositional defiant disorder.

What are sleep difficulties?

Many children with Tourette Syndrome have difficulties with sleep. This includes difficulties such as going to bed on their own and problems getting off to sleep. The sleep difficulties may be so severe that they disrupt everyone in the family home.

The owl and the pussy cat

The small owl and the pussy cat went to see
The doctors at hospital one day
They took some honey, and plenty of money,
While their parents listened to what the docs did say.

My obsessions are thoughts going round and round
In my head, over and over: how silly it must sound,
My compulsions make me do lots of things too,
Like lining up shoes, being 'just right', kissing you!

With my ADHD I have poor concentration,
My mind wanders off, I have no attention,
I can't wait for things, and so must butt in,
I'm 'going' all the time, too full of action.

Sometimes I get sad and just cry all the time,
I feel all these problems are really only mine,
I can't even sleep and I don't want to eat,
I don't enjoy anything, not even a nice treat.

Mary M. Robertson
With apologies to Edward Lear

Chapter 4

How do doctors treat and support young people with Tourette Syndrome?

For many years it was thought that there was no treatment apart from a talking treatment called psychoanalysis. This is no longer used for the treatment of TS except in very special cases where the doctors are specially trained. Nowadays the doctors realise that educating their patients even if they are young people is important. It is also important to 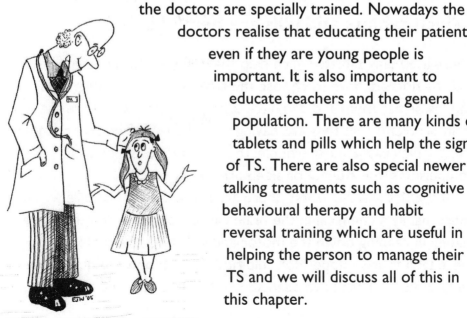 educate teachers and the general population. There are many kinds of tablets and pills which help the signs of TS. There are also special newer talking treatments such as cognitive behavioural therapy and habit reversal training which are useful in helping the person to manage their TS and we will discuss all of this in this chapter.

What do you mean by education about TS?

We feel it is important that young people with TS understand their condition. If somebody understands something, it is much easier to do something about it. So we like telling our young patients with TS that they are not alone and that many other youngsters have TS. We think it is important that young people know that usually TS gets better with age and that often people learn to cope with it. It is also important for everybody to understand that TS was once thought to be uncommon and now it is thought to be much more common.

Remember that TS occurs in all parts of the world, which shows that it is to do with our bodies rather than our culture. It is important to know that there is help for the young person with TS and that there are tablets and other therapies which are useful.

Some youngsters with TS struggle with school and these people may need extra help there. In the same way as teaching the young person with TS about his or her condition, it is important that mums, dads and teachers also know about TS so that they know how to help young people with TS.

Which tablets and pills are helpful in TS?

There are many tablets which help the various different signs of TS and the doctors have to choose the tablets after the young person and his or her mum and dad have told the doctor which are the main problems that they are having with their TS. The doctor must know which cause most trouble: the tics, the obsessions and compulsions, the ADHD or sleep problems.

If the tics are the worst, there are some tablets and pills which affect mainly a chemical in the brain called dopamine and these are helpful in calming down the motor and vocal tics. Examples of these tablets are haloperidol, sulpiride, risperidone and quetiapine. Only some of these have been shown by doctors to be better than sugar pills in some research which doctors call 'double blind trials'. This is where the patient takes a tablet and does not know whether it has medicine in it or whether it has sugar in it (known as a placebo). The doctor checking whether the tics are better also does not know what is in the tablet. In other words the patient and the doctor are 'blind' to the contents of the tablet. Medicines that are shown to be effective include haloperidol, pimozide, sulpiride, tiapride and risperidone. The very new pills have only been used in small numbers of patients and therefore only doctors with a lot of experience tend to prescribe them. Unfortunately many of the tablets have side effects which often make the person with TS feel horrible. These pills may make young people feel tired, a bit sad, put on weight and have joint pains. Some of these tablets also affect chemicals in our body such as prolactin and sugar and we know that many of our doctor colleagues take a blood test to make sure they know what our normal prolactin and sugar levels are before the treatment starts. Do not be scared as blood tests do not always hurt as many of the people who take blood, called phlebotomists, use a local anaesthetic (special cream) which stops the pain by numbing the skin.

In those young people with TS with mainly obsessions and compulsions, some of the tablets which affect serotonin may be given. Examples of these include clomipramine, fluoxetine, fluvoxamine, sertraline and citalopram. As many of these tablets are not really recommended in children with other disorders, the doctor prescribing them has to have read the medical books and know both the good and bad effects of these tablets.

For those young people with TS and ADHD (see Chapter 3), other types of tablets are given. The older types include clonidine and guanfacine (not generally used, in the UK). Stimulants such as methylphenidate can be used, but in some young people it can cause an increase in tics and therefore the doctor, patient and parents must be on the look-out for any new tics or an increase in tics. Some doctors have used clonidine and a stimulant. A new tablet called atomoxetine has been licensed for ADHD in some parts of the world and it seems that this may well be useful in young people with TS and ADHD.

Tell me about cognitive behaviour therapy

Cognitive behaviour therapy (CBT) is a type of talking therapy which aims to reduce psychological distress by altering the way we think. It looks at how we think, how we feel and what we do. It is sometimes used by doctors to help young people with depression and behaviour such as obsessions and compulsions (see Chapter 3). Some therapists believe that CBT is helpful in reducing tics. However, there has been no conclusive evidence that tics are reduced and much more research is needed to say that CBT may be helpful.

Tell me about habit reversal training

This is a treatment that is only carried out by specialist therapists who work with patients, usually adults with TS. It involves the patient being trained to be aware of the early signs of a tic and then teaching the person to contract the opposite muscle to the one affected by the tic. For example, if the tic causes the arm to move out, push the hand down onto the thigh. The evidence for this therapy working is not great and many more studies are needed before we can recommend this treatment to our patients.

Are there any other kind of therapies?

Psychotherapy

This is a talking therapy which might make you feel better about having TS but does not affect the tics in any way. We only recommend it if there are other problems such as relationship difficulties.

Family supportive psychotherapy

This therapy involves the whole family being seen and talking about problems in the family. Again, it will not affect the tics in any way but may help families deal with difficult issues.

Are there any organisations for young people with TS?

There are several organisations across the world dealing with TS. These organisations are usually run by people who have TS or know someone who does.

They can provide information and fact sheets. Usually there are newsletters with interesting things about TS such as day trips, poems or simply people telling their stories. Occasionally they organise groups, holidays and camp trips.

TOURETTE SYNDROME ASSOCIATION UK

Membership number: 576

Who treats the young person with TS?

Many professionals can be involved in helping young people with TS and we have put their names and what they do in the box below.

Who is involved?

General Practitioner the local family doctor

Child Psychiatrist sees children and adolescents for lots of reasons including emotional and behavioural difficulties

Paediatrician doctor who looks after children

Psychologist helps with assessment, investigations and talking treatment

Special Educational Needs Coordinator (SENCO) a teacher who is responsible for helping children who have medical or behavioural difficulties in the classroom

School Nurse nurse who helps with medical problems in school

Counsellor helps with talking treatment and support

Jabberwocky

Beware the Jabberwock, my dear son
But not the doctors – who you mustn't shun
They can help your hyper, and your tics
And also your OCD – they'll try and fix.

They'll give lots of support, and maybe pills
And Habit Reversal Training may help your ills
There's CBT, and some good talking treatment too
They will also suggest the great TSAs to you.

Mary M. Robertson
With apologies to Lewis Carroll

Chapter 5

How will I cope in school?

Introduction

Life in school can be pretty lousy at times. Teachers are telling you what to do, complicated homework, bullying, peer pressure and the dreaded parents' evening. What about if you also have TS? Will anyone notice? How will the teacher react? Will you cope with the workload?

We feel that school-time difficulties should be taken seriously and talked about. If you are worried about anything in school then it might be helpful to talk to Mum and Dad about it.

Should people at school know that I have Tourette Syndrome?

Many young people are ashamed of their tics and therefore do not want it to be given a name or labelled at school. But we have found that many more children actually like to give a name for their tics. Why? This is because once a diagnosis is made they and their parents feel that they are not alone. In fact, as we have said, there are literally thousands of other young people with tics and TS. When their parents decide where to send them to school, they have to decide whether the school should be aware of the problem or not. Some parents are protective of their children and do not want to give them a 'label' – as this sometimes leads to them being shunned by the other pupils. This is called a stigma. This stigma may reduce the young person's self-confidence if it is not handled in a caring way. No child really wants to be different from his or her classmates. But if a child is suffering with upset emotions, or not doing as well at school as they hoped, then it is usually good for the school to be told of their TS as they can then get help. You can talk to Mum and Dad about this and if possible make a joint decision – that's the way some of the best decisions in life are made – with someone else's help and guidance.

Should Mum, Dad and the teacher talk to each other?

With parents' permission, doctors can write letters to schools to tell teachers about children with TS and some of the problems which they may have. If Mum and Dad can also talk to the teacher, then this may help even more. For example, the parents may let the teacher know exactly about what pills the child is taking. It is a good idea for the doctor also to write a brief letter to the school every time there is a change to the pills. This of course has to be done with the parents' permission again.

Teachers are useful observers of children's progress with medication, as the teachers see the children for several hours a day and during this time the children are either learning or mixing with other children. Although parents of course know their children very well, often they see their children when they are alone at home, in company they know well, out doing nice things such as being in the park or watching TV or playing with a game boy, or, of course, at night, when hopefully they are asleep most of the time! But teachers see them in the day when they are surrounded by other children and trying to concentrate. Teachers therefore need to know about uncomfortable side effects such as being sleepy, a bit moody and maybe even not wanting to go to school, even if they usually like school.

It is a good idea for mums and dads to have a meeting with the teachers before the start of each new school year. Although teachers can pass information from one year to the next, a 'face-to-face' meeting makes it friendlier. Later in the year another meeting can be arranged including others such as the school psychologist, occupational therapist and nurse – especially if the child is taking pills.

How can the child help the teacher? The young person can tell the teacher if they are feeling good or bad, better or worse and if they have any problems. *However,* all young people are naughty from time to time, and young people with TS must not blame their naughtiness on TS. Many young people with TS are children and we do not want to blame TS when the young person and not their TS is to blame. The young person should always try to be open and honest and tell the truth.

What does the teacher need to know?

The teacher should be aware that stress could make the tics worse. Exam time is often very difficult. Often when the young person has to read or talk aloud in the class the tics are also very bad. This can be when the young person has to recite poems, take part in plays, talk in assembly or answer questions in front of the class or school.

We do understand that it is difficult to get the 'balance right' about performing in public. If the young person is worried about speaking in public because of his or her tics, then making him or her the centre of attention is not going to help. Some people, even adults, are scared of public speaking as they are not very good at it – and they don't even have TS! But avoiding normal school experiences is not good either. The best way of doing things is probably to talk to the teacher or to Mum and Dad. Remember that there may be many actors and performers out there, whom we think have got tics and even TS, who would not have made a career of acting if they were held back when it came to public performances at school.

Depending on how you and your parents feel, it is sometimes a good idea for the other pupils to learn about tics and TS. If you feel brave enough, it might be useful to give a short presentation to the class on TS and what it is like to have TS. You will have read some young people's stories already and seen how amazing they are.

What can I do to help myself with the work in school?

Breaking down projects into smaller bits over shorter periods of time will help the young person with ADHD stay on task and finish the work. For example, if a child has one term to complete and hand in a geography project, break the project down into smaller parts to be done every week. As an example, background reading needs to be done by week one, the introduction needs to be written up by week two, the method written up by week three.

Homework

For many young people with TS, the last thing they want to do at the end of a stressful day at school is more work – homework. The child usually feels tired as well as having had enough. If homework has to be done, then there are some ways of making it more pleasant.

As said before, break the work into small chunks and teachers should know that not all of the work will get done. Use homework diaries to organise the pupil. Make sure the teacher of each lesson has seen that the homework to be done has been written down in the diary. This avoids 'forgetting' to write it down. Another way to make sure homework is done is to see if you can do the homework for the morning lessons during the lunch break. This can be done in the library or in a special classroom. This is helpful if you are easily distracted by siblings at home. It also helps keep you out of trouble during the lunch break at school.

Useful tips for parents/carers on how to approach children's homework

The teacher and parents should decide together when is the best time for the pupil to do the homework: some children like to relax first, others like to start when they get home from school.

Parents should find a place away from distractions: some kids like to have some background noise, others prefer quiet.

Avoid clutter on desks or table surfaces.

Remember TV programmes can be recorded so that your child can see them after he or she has finished their homework!

Exams

Many examination boards are very understanding and, with planning and letters of support from your doctor or psychologist, simple changes can be made to make exam time a bit less stressful than it already is. Usually examination boards allow your usual method of working in the classroom to be continued in the examination hall. So if you use a laptop in a particular lesson, then you should be allowed to use the laptop in that particular exam.

The important thing to remember is to make applications for special arrangements for exams as early as possible, with supportive letters from teachers and specialists involved such as psychologists and doctors. Other changes or modifications include allowing extra time to take tests, providing movement and breaks during exams, and allowing the young person to sit the exam in a special quiet room with a person watching (called invigilators) so that they do not feel stressed about themselves or worried about their noises disturbing the other children. The young person may also be allowed to respond verbally or by speaking and being allowed the use of a word processor.

What if I am bullied?

If you are being called names, the first thing to do is to ignore it. Bullies usually want some sort of reaction and by ignoring any initial teasing you may bring about an end to the name calling. If things continue, however, then it is important to talk to someone such as your parents or class teacher. Writing things down

may help – you can even write a poem about it, but please do not keep it to yourself. Show Mum and Dad.

Talk to your friends. They may be in a similar position. If you have no friends then it is very important to talk to the teachers and Mum and Dad.

If you feel there is simply no one you can talk to, then you can always get help from national organisations that help children, such as Childline in the UK: their website is www.childline.org.uk, or alternatively phone 0800-1111 (free 24 hours).

What is a statement?

All schools in the United Kingdom should have a policy to make sure that all pupils learn properly. If they have special educational needs then this must be recognised and steps taken to help the pupil. If the school is unable to provide help then schools should apply for resources or funds for that pupil. The help needed may be the supplying of special reading material (e.g. big print books), the use of a laptop or by providing a support teacher for several hours during the week. Different countries will have different policies for providing resources.

Songs of innocence

Playing down in schools, some so wild
Singing sweet songs of pleasant glee
In the playground I then saw a child
And he was laughing and said to me:

'I've got TS, so don't think I'm mad
I'm not really naughty or indeed very bad,
I've got many tics and other problems too
So let me tell you now – just what to do:

'My doctor will write and say what's wrong
Try to include me – please let me belong
Let me use a computer in my exams,
And I will write better – without my hands.

'And give a quiet room, or some extra time
And then I will do my exams just fine
And I'll pass the test, please Mum and Dad,
Then – we'll say thanks to you, and not think I'm bad'

Mary M. Robertson
With apologies to William Blake

Chapter 6

What are the life stories of brothers, sisters, parents and young people around the world with Tourette Syndrome?

STORIES OF YOUNG PEOPLE WITH TOURETTE SYNDROME

Names have been changed for confidentiality reasons.

Tom, aged 13 (UK)

Determined

When you have a problem
And it's called Tourette's
You have to learn to live with it
Just like other pets.

So try to be determined
It might just go away
Try to learn to live with it
Really start to play.

If you'll be determined
Don't waste your life away
Go out and enjoy yourself
Learn to play, play, play.

My name is ***
And I have Tourette's
Now I have to live with it
But the syndrome is for LET.

Reprinted with kind permission from the Tourette Syndrome (UK) Association

Luca, aged 13 (UK)

I used to think that all books talking about my habits were rubbish and couldn't help me. Taking the time to read about other people with similar problems, it does help. You're not the only one with these problems. All you need to do to find that out is to look around you. I think of my habits as hiccups, I feel I don't want to do it but I have to. If I don't, it's like I'm going to explode.

Sophie, aged 11 (UK)

The first time I heard of the word Tourette was when I went to see some doctors in a hospital in London and they explained to me what it was. I have never felt different to my friends, but when I have a new habit some friends ask me, 'Why do you keep on doing that?' Sometimes nobody notices what I am doing.

Teachers did not really notice that I had habits until I had a really bad time at school with my tests and it started to get more obvious.

I have had lots of different habits but I do not remember when they started although it was some time ago. Some of my habits have been words and some have been twitches.

Some of the words that I can remember saying over and over again are 'sorry' and at another time 'thank you'. The first one I can remember saying was 'doh'. I know that I am doing it, but sometimes I cannot stop. Sometimes it can be embarrassing.

I don't always realize that I have a new habit until I find that I am doing something over and over again.

The habits are worse when I am tired or stressed about something. They also happen when I relax.

Some habits are annoying to others like when I click my fingers, or when I keep repeating words.

Although I have this problem, I like sports and my favourite games are rugby and netball. I play rugby for my local club and netball for my school team.

My habits seem to be getting better as I get older. My worst time so far was when I was in Year 5.

I used to find it hard to talk about what I do, but then the doctors told me why I have my habits. I feel better knowing that there are other people with the same problem.

I still feel like a normal kid except for a few strange habits.

Ben, aged 15 (USA)

Hi, my name is Ben and I live in New Mexico in the USA. I am 15 years old and I was diagnosed with Tourette Syndrome when I was 8, in the second grade. I was hit very hard with Tourette Syndrome and my tics were really bad. I was in a private school and I suddenly could not do the things I used to be able to do, like reading and writing. Everything got really hard for me. At first the doctors did not know what was wrong, and I thought I might have a brain tumour. Once we found it was Tourette, my family and I were greatly relieved because you do not die from this.

Everybody was really nice to me in my school. My classmates and teachers were very understanding. They would read and write with me and help me with all kinds of things. School got too hard and eventually I was unable to go to school for a while. My mom took me to see a doctor on the east coast to see if he could help me. We started medication but it really did not help my tics. My mom went to a conference on Tourette and learnt about it. Then my family got involved with the National Tourette Syndrome Association. My mom began a chapter in New Mexico for TSA, in order to begin educating people in our state about TS.

I started public school in the fourth grade and I was put into a classroom with other children that were very different from me. The school was not willing to learn about TS. The kids teased me in the playground and my teacher did not know how to teach me. They did not think I was very smart. I started getting really stressed with school and hated going to school. At school no one understood the difficulties that I was dealing with. When I was at home I was hard to live with. I have two brothers and a sister. I took much of my stress and anger out on my family. It was really hard on my siblings and my mom and dad. There were a lot of things that I needed that the school would not help me with. It got so bad we had to go to court. We won the court case and I was placed in a much better environment, a gifted classroom for kids with challenges. This was great. The school wanted to learn about me and Tourette. They set me up with a computer and some good software. The software reads to me and I am able to speak into the computer and have it type for me. The teachers kept my homework level low. As the stress went down my tics got better. My mom did talks for the teachers on TS and I did them for the kids in my classes. Everything got so much better when everybody around me understood Tourette. I started being able to do things that I really enjoy.

Along with my Tourette, I have OCD, or obsessive compulsive disorder, which can be lots worse than my tics now. I take medication for my OCD and it really helps. One of the doctors I went to see was in New York. While I was in New York, I visited the National TSA. This was so cool. It was exciting to see people out there researching and educating others about TS. My mom and I go to the National TSA conference every other year. This gives me the chance to meet others that are coping with the same difficulties that I am. I met Jim Eisenreich, a famous baseball player, one year and he signed a baseball for me. He has TS and does just fine.

I really enjoy high school. I believe that people with TS can be anything they want to be. TS does not have me, it is only a small part of me. I am just like any other kid. Sometimes I run into a challenge that I have to be creative in coping with. I plan on going to college and then to graduate school. I have a real interest in animals and genetic engineering.

Buster, aged 14 (UK)

Life with Tourette Syndrome

My name is Buster, I am 14 years old and I have an illness called Tourette Syndrome. My TS is shown in many different ways. I spit, twitch, blink, nod my head, flick my arm, clench my jaw, twitch my leg, sniff and chew paper. You name it, I do it. I have had TS since I was 5 and at that point it wasn't bad, but as I've got older it's become more noticeable and it bothers me more. When I was 10 I decided I really wanted to get rid of TS. I felt like this because when I played for my old football team I gave away a penalty kick, not because I deliberately fouled the player, but I flicked my arm outwards and to the referee it looked as though I was trying to punch the player near to me, but I wasn't. It was my TS and the referee didn't understand so I really felt bad. The TS followed with bad behaviour at school, silly behaviour and reckless behaviour. You don't understand what you have done until you have done it. After the 'silly behaviour spell', life was back to normal for some time without doing anything wrong and I was getting to live with TS until something really bad happened. I was out of control, I didn't understand anything. I am not going to tell you what happened, but let me tell you it was stupid. I feel depressed, trapped, upset and strange, and I hope things get back to normal. I know I can't blame it all on TS but I am sure that my actions have been to do with TS.

Nellie, aged 15 (Australia)

In the eyes of a child

In the eyes of a child
Every day is worth living
Every sin is worth forgiving

In the eyes of a child
Nothing can go wrong
And even harsh words can seem like a song

In the eyes of a child
Everyone is the same
And no-one needs to be ashamed – TS is just a name

I wish I saw everything through the eyes of a child
If I saw everything so black and white
Then maybe happiness would not seem so out of sight

Matthew, aged 9 (UK)

Hi, my name is Matthew. I'm 9 years old and I have Tourette Syndrome.

My story started about two years ago. I had a nasty cough and a cold that I couldn't get rid of, even though my mum took me to the doctor's and I had lots of medicines. When I did eventually get rid of the cough and cold, I was left with a 'gulping' sound, which I felt I had to do, even though there was no real reason for me to do it.

A short time passed and I started to blink my eyes very fast and make big frowns. Some of my school friends found this funny, because when I frowned, my whole scalp moved forward – something which I cannot do now, even when thinking about it! After this, I started moving my whole head and neck in an 'S' shape. Sometimes my school friends would moan at me and tell me to stop doing it, but I couldn't stop it and I had no control over what I was doing. I don't think they believed me.

This seemed to go on for months. Mum took me back to the doctor's several times and I was sent to the local children's hospital. The worst bit about going there was that I had to have a blood test. Even though they put on some magic cream before they did the blood test, I still didn't like having it done. I also had a CT brain scan. This wasn't painful but I had to lie still on a bed for about 30 minutes, as I went inside a big tunnel and the machine made some strange sounds. All my tests came back normal which was good in a way, but I still didn't know what was the matter with me.

Mum had a feeling that she knew what the problem was, and so Mum and Dad took me to see a consultant in London who is a specialist in tics. The consultant saw me and was really nice. He said I had Tourette Syndrome. Shortly after seeing him, I started taking some tablets called clonidine to help me cope with my movements. During this time my movements kept changing. One of the hardest things to deal with was not knowing what movements I was going to have, and when I was going to have them. The movements I have had included tapping on tables and desks, my leg twitching and kicking out under the table, arms being stretched out suddenly and shaking them and making a funny 'mmmm' sound. My mum asked my teacher to tell the other Year 4 children what my problem was and she did. Now I have friends who do not make fun of my movements and sounds and they stand up for me if anyone says anything horrible to me.

At Christmas-time we went to Florida. I remember that at teatime on Christmas Day, my legs suddenly went from under me and I would have hit the floor, had Mum not been straight behind me. Things seemed to get worse from here on. During the rest of our holiday I had lots of these movements and this meant that I couldn't go into the swimming pool unless Mum or Dad was right next to me, as they were worried that if my legs went funny again I could go under the water.

When we got back to England, I went to see the specialist doctor again and he changed my tablets to sulpiride. I also stopped doing PE at school as I was so tired and found it difficult to cope with staying awake sometimes. I went to bed even earlier than usual, but this still didn't help. My teacher is great and very understanding and often gives me a hug when I need one. I also leave the room sometimes, so I can go and let off some steam when things feel really bad. I also get lots of headaches.

Over the next few months my movements stayed pretty much the same. My arms and legs would all of a sudden shoot out, and I would thrash around at home as though I was a fish being fried! Sometimes I would laugh afterwards, sometimes I would cry, as my elbow and knee joints became painful. Mum takes me to see some osteopaths (specialists who are not doctors but who help with bone and muscle problems) and they help me relax. They are great and I have a real laugh with them. I look forward to seeing them every few weeks.

During the Easter holidays my movements changed yet again – this time they became more frightening for me. I started to hit my head with my fists at first. Then I tried to hit my head on corners of tables and walls, on the floor and on the fireplace. Dinnertime can be quite entertaining as I keep trying to grab the cutlery and poke myself in the eyes if Mum and Dad aren't quick enough! For some reason I also started to feel frightened of my movements and would curl up in a ball and make a sound like an injured dog – a sort of whimpering sound. I still don't understand why I do this or why I am frightened. Mum and Dad try to talk me out of doing these things and try to distract me. Sometimes this works, but sometimes the feeling is so strong that I cannot stop doing it and they have to actually pull me away from the wall or take the knife and fork out of my hands by force. This is what upsets me the most, as I know I shouldn't be doing these things, but I can't stop it all the same. I know they are only doing things to stop me from really hurting myself, but I still wish they would let me, as this is the only way that I feel a sense of relief.

At the time of writing this, I am struggling to concentrate. This is common for me. I try to keep my movements under control and spend so much energy on doing this that I get really twitchy, and they have to come out then, no matter what. This is why the evenings at home are often worse than my time at school. Lately though, my movements have been so bad that I haven't been able to hold them in at school and I think sometimes they might scare my classmates. I have just started taking a stress ball to school with me as I find that I can concentrate a bit better when I am holding it.

I have found a new friend who lives in the same town as me and also has TS. He is 12 years old and I am really pleased that I have met him, as I can talk to him about what I do and how I feel, and we both relax so that our movements come out and it doesn't matter, as we are both the same.

I went to see two more specialists who work together recently. They said to me that 'I wasn't mad and I wasn't bad'. I also have something called attention deficit hyperactivity disorder (ADHD) which makes me fidgety and I find it hard to concentrate. I also have obsessive compulsive behaviour (OCB), where I collect things and put them in my pockets. Mum and I laugh about this, as she usually finds stones and twigs and bits of rubbish when she checks my pockets before washing my clothes. I usually have lucky straws which aren't really that lucky, as they keep getting thrown away! Mum and Dad used to put me to bed, and when Mum made my bed in the morning she used to find three torches under my pillow – I used to sneak out of bed later and get them out of my drawer and put them under my pillow. Mum and Dad and I always laugh about this. At the moment I put a watch under my pillow at night because I feel I need to. The specialist doctors changed my tablets yet again. This one is called risperidone and will hopefully help my movements.

Unfortunately my school are worried about my movements where I hurt myself. I think they are worried that I might accidentally hurt someone else and so I am hoping I can move to a special school from September. They are used to helping children with problems and have a boy with TS already there. It is a really nice school and they only have about eight children in each class, with two or three teachers. Fingers crossed I can go there.

We were supposed to go to see friends in Spain at Easter for a big party, but we had to cancel because I couldn't cope being around lots of people whom I didn't know. I also couldn't go to Cub Camp, because they couldn't be sure that I would be safe when I had my movements. I really wish that I didn't have TS. I don't like being different and I don't like the problems I have because of my movements.

Mum has explained why I may have TS. I know they haven't got a cure for it yet, but I am hoping they will have one day.

I can't really remember not having my movements now. They seem to have been with me forever. It hasn't made any difference knowing what my problem was called. I'm still the same person. I know that my mum and dad, nans and grandads, aunts and uncles still love me.

Written with the help of Matthew's mother

Daniel, aged 14 (UK)

Hi, I've had Tourette Syndrome (TS) almost all my life. I was diagnosed with it when I was about 9 years old. The first sign of me having TS was when I was about 4 and a half years old and it was when I had just got home from school and I sat down in front of the TV with my legs crossed and I started to rock backwards and forwards. My mum told me to stop it and I said, 'What? I'm not doing anything!' So my mum just ignored me, and that was my first sign of having TS.

Because I've had TS for quite a long time, I've learnt how to live with it and how to cope with it. Although I've learnt how to cope with it, I still have lots of problems at school such as bullying. I was bullied when I was in junior school and I am still bullied now. I get people calling me names and copying my tics. When I was about 7 years old I decided to join my local football club, but I had problems there as well. Because I was excited my tics were quite bad and some of the kids at the club started to make fun of me, but I tried my hardest to ignore them. But there was one person who really got to me, and that was one of the football coaches himself. I got really upset when one of the football coaches started calling me 'Quackers' which I didn't find very funny. I was very upset, and told my mum. She spoke to the leader and he didn't believe her, so I had to give up football.

One of the tics I had was very strange; as I was walking along I stopped and rocked backwards and forwards as if my foot was stuck to the ground. Because of this my five-minute walk to school turned into a half-hour walk, which was very frustrating. I've had quite a few arm tics as well, one of which frightened me. It was a tic where I shot my arm out to the side. The reason I said it frightened me was because when my family and I were sitting at the dinner table having our dinner my arm shot out to the side with my fork in my hand and I was afraid that I would accidentally stab my mum with the fork. Thankfully that tic has served its time with me and has passed on. WAHOO!

I am 14 and in Year 10. You might be thinking that this is a bit young for a Year 10 pupil, but I am one of the youngest in the year. I have just taken my mock GCSEs and I found them quite hard. I have been very stressed out because of the exams and because of this my tics have been very bad. My arm tics have been OK but it was my face tics that were bad. I've had several face tics due to the exams, one of which has been extremely annoying. It's one where I frown and shut my eyes. I find it annoying because it makes my face muscles really ache.

I have several hobbies in which I need a fair bit of concentration. They are both to do with controlling radio-controlled (r-c) vehicles. My main one I have at the moment is that I am a member of my local r-c car club, where we race with top-class cars. At the moment, my facial tics are quite bad for some reason, and when I race I quite often lose sight and lose control of the car due to my facial tics. We are spending a lot of money trying to fix the car, because it is so expensive to fix. My other r-c hobby that I've only just started is radio-controlled helicopters. Flying the helicopter is more difficult than driving the car and therefore needs more concentration. My tics make it extremely difficult to learn to fly the 'copter because I lose sight of it when my facial tics 'come on' so it crashes.

So all in all, TS is quite annoying at times, but I've learnt to live with it. I mean, we've all got to some time because it will most probably be a part of me forever. At other times I quite enjoy having it because I've been on TV talking about it, so it can be very rewarding in some circumstances.

Kyle (USA)

My name is Kyle and I have Tourette Syndrome plus. The plus stands for OCD, obsessive compulsive disorder. Having TS made it hard to work in school. I had bad muscle spasms, especially in my hands, making it hard to learn to write. I had more trouble with concentrating, vocalisations and anger when I got frustrated, which was most of the time. My OCD made me do things over and over until I thought they were perfect. I would be afraid that if things were not perfect, I would get into big trouble or people would chop off my head or something. So most of the time, I did not finish my work and then I would get into trouble. Timed tests were a nightmare. My parents had me put on medication, but it made me sleepy and it made my tics worse or did not do anything at all. Nowadays I barely tic at all and I am not on any medication.

My principal did not think that TS existed and these are her own words: 'Tourette is just an excuse for bad parenting.' My parents sent her tapes on TS but she never looked at them. Some of the teachers at my school believed my parents and had heard of TS. One day I was at school and had a bad anger outburst and my principal was going to kick me out of school. She even called the cops, but then my parents said 'no' and took me out, so now I am taught at home.

Other people think that if I have TS, then I must use profanities and that I cannot control it. But only a small percentage of kids with TS do that. Sometimes people think that TS is like the flu or a cold and you can catch it. And most difficult of all is when I am around people like that, I can control myself and then they think that I am lying about having TS at all.

Last April I was invited to go to a TS camp in Texas and saw kids who had worse tics than me. One kid in my group had very bad mood swings. He would be happy sometimes, but mostly he would always be angry or sad about something. Another kid in my group had a strange tic. Every now and then he would look like he was screaming but with no sound and he would not even recall that he was doing it. Apparently one of my counsellors had a tic. He would bark like a dog and then stop. I did not even notice this. My favourite things about camp were rock climbing, horse riding, archery, the animal barn, and swimming in the pool.

I have written three cookbooks. Ten per cent of the profit of all books goes to the Tourette Syndrome Association to find a cure. My dad and I are also working on two books together. I also come up with other book ideas. The point is that I have TS but it does not slow me down, and its only the people that do not understand it that think it makes me a bad kid.

Emma, aged 13 (UK)

Funny shakes, a chicken and Tourette Probably Syndrome

I'm 13-year-old Emma, and a few days ago, I found out that I had Tourette Syndrome. It all started one Tuesday in June, at the end of lunch.

The bell for the end of lunch had gone, and as I was heading in for physics, I felt a weird twitching in the upper half of my body. It made me really tired, and I felt really bad as people, especially the not-so-nice people, kept staring at me, and making jokes among themselves. I knew they were looking at me; after all, it had always been them. Let me explain. In November, I suddenly had a fit of coughing, while in a restaurant with the rest of the special junior choir. We were out of school, due to the fact that we had been given the chance to sing at the Royal Albert Hall. Anyway, after about half an hour, when we were back in our dressing room, the coughing had stopped. I forgot about it, thinking it was just a reaction to cold ice cream. We went and sung for the crowds and then were collected by our parents to go home. One of my music teachers explained to my mum about the cough and it didn't seem to affect me for the rest of the night. But it did keep appearing every so often for the rest of the year, and even into the next year. After two doses of antibiotics, I saw a doctor, who said it was a post viral cough and gave me an inhaler.

In school, as you might expect, people use deodorants and so on to stop them from smelling bad after PE. Even though sprays are not allowed, people don't seem to care. Soon, I discovered that deodorant set my coughing off, and I had to use the inhaler to stop it. This went on for a while, until a teacher found out, and told them off. They then asked: 'If deodorants set you off coughing, then what do you use?'

'Have you ever heard of roll on? It's what we're supposed to use in school, if we need to,' I answered; after all, it was true. They pulled a false smile, and I walked past them.

A few weeks later, it started again. At the start of the RS lesson, before the teacher arrived, they decided to spray themselves, or rather their clothes, right behind me, even though one of their friends kept reminding them about me, and telling them not to. Surprise, surprise, it set the cough off again.

Anyway, back to Tuesday. I was sat with my friends. I could tell they were freaked out by this twitch, as they looked at me strangely when one happened and kept asking me if I was OK. Of course I was, except for the tight feeling in my chest that was relieved when a twitch had finished, the bad feeling in my tummy and feeling very, very tired! After the last lesson of the day, I walked round to the music studio. As the twitching had not yet gone away, I could not play my cello properly, so at four o'clock I decided to phone my mum to pick me up. My mum took me immediately to the doctor's. He said he had never seen anything like it, but thought maybe it could be a tic. He rang the hospital, who said to bring me in. When we arrived at the hospital, we waited for about an hour, and when I was seen, I had a blood test done, but as it was so busy, by the time the doctor came back, I'd stopped shaking but a strange hiccup noise had replaced it. As the doctors were still unsure, they decided to keep me in the children's ward.

I was diagnosed with Spinal Myoclonus. I had an ECG to see if I was able to take the drugs, and then I was able to go home. I was given Epilim and clonazepam to treat it.

On Monday morning of the following week, I went to see the doctor at SOS hospital. The clonazepam was making me feel really happy and then really sad, but I felt fine in myself. I couldn't understand why I kept changing my mood, although I was mostly really depressed. Because of these side effects to the drug he took me off them and sent me down for an MRI scan. It was not very nice as it was like a big smartie tube. I had to go in three times and even though I had ear plugs in it was really noisy. After the first and second scans on my brain and neck, my mum told me to think of something I would really like to do, so for some very weird reason, I thought of holding a chicken. After the last scan on my spine, my mum took me to Chicken's Farm where I got to hold my chicken. I held a Rhode Island red cockerel named Richard and a hen with no name. It really cheered me up.

On Tuesday I felt a lot better and on Wednesday afternoon I went back to school. On Wednesday morning I went to see the doctor again and he was pleased to see that I was feeling better.

Things went smoothly for the next day, so on Friday I got to go on my Year 8 French trip. We went to Nausica and Saint Omer and the shaking only got bad as we were leaving, because I was tired. I felt so happy that I had got to go on the French trip because before I had been worried I would not go.

On Wednesday 6th July I went to see the doctor for a check-up. He said I was OK still, but in the afternoon things changed. In the lesson after lunch my legs turned to jelly and I couldn't walk. I felt really bad as things had been going really well. I was sent home and my legs went back to normal and I got an appointment for the next day to see the doctor again. When I got to the hospital, however, the doctor was not there as SOS hospital had been put on red alert because of the London bombings. An appointment was arranged for the next day with a new doctor. Her name was Dr Shoes.

When I saw Dr Shoes, my legs got very bad as I felt very nervous. At the end of the appointment she told us that I would have to stay at another hospital, on Thursday 14th. I really did not want to go into hospital again.

On the Thursday that I was due to go into hospital, my mum and I drove. We were slightly late, but it did not matter as Dr Shoes was doing rounds at the hospital anyway. When she saw us she was with a French doctor, who said that I definitely had tic disorder. She also said that the cough was a tic. She sounded very sure and because the diagnosis had changed I was taken off the Epilim. And I also did not have to stay in hospital after all. I was really pleased, but Dr Shoes said to come back later so that she could ask me some questions.

I had lunch in the waiting area in the hospital and then went back to the consulting room. Dr Shoes asked me questions while she got an assistant to film me. They filmed me for new medical students.

On Monday 18th July, I went to my dad's graduation. I really enjoyed it and all through the day my tic was fine.

However, when we went for a meal with my dad's friend, I began coughing again. It calmed down on the way home.

On Monday 5th September I went back to the hospital. Every so often I had bad shaking sessions, but apart from that everything was back to normal. I saw two neurologists, two psychologists and Professor Robertson. I was asked a lot about 'habits' and family life until we all grouped together at the end. Professor Robertson said that it was probably Tourette Syndrome. She gave me a lot of information and told me that it was very common. She also said that by the age of 18, 50 per cent of people with TS stop 50 per cent of their tics.

So there you have it, I've told you about the funny shakes, the chicken and Tourette Probably Syndrome.

SIBLINGS' STORIES

Helen (UK)

Dear Tourette Syndrome Association,

I'm H, my brother J has Tourette Syndrome. I'd really like to hear from other brothers or sisters of people with TS. I'm very proud of some things he has done but I've also wanted to kill him more times than is natural.

His list of strange behaviour includes: whacking a friend of mine over the head with a Christmas decoration, throwing bowling balls down lanes before the machine is switched on for our game. And wading into a duck pond waist-deep wearing trainers, tracksuit bottoms and a T-shirt.

Having said that, he can be a perfectly normal, charming kid to have around. Really – until he asks, 'Am I normal? Do I seem normal to you?'

As a sister of a sufferer of TS (fondly known in my family as T-rex or Tough Sh** syndrome) I've had a rough time. I've had all the 'yer brother's mental' in the playground, I'm the one he swings for when he's angry and I'm not the one that the family guidance lady is there to see. So, like I said, I'd really appreciate it if other sisters or brothers of people with TS would write in. WE NEED A SUPPORT GROUP!!!

Luckily when J isn't being nuts he can have a good sense of humour. Which is why he let me make his 'freak-o-meter!': cut out the 'J' counter and put it where you think he is. From 'too nice, unreal' to 'OFF THE SCALES!!!'.

All in all, he's very unpredictable but he can be nice. However, catch us on a bad day and you'll hear me screaming at him to drop dead.

Does this sound familiar?

Reprinted with kind permission from the Tourette Syndrome (UK) Association

Mia, aged 13 (UK)

What it feels like to have a sister with Tourette Syndrome

My sister Sophie is 11 and she has Tourette Syndrome. It was such a relief when we finally found a name for what she was doing and she wasn't just crazy. She has had these random habits for quite a while now but we had no idea what they were or how to deal with it.

When it got bad and her habits started to happen more and become more noticeable in public, it became embarrassing but I also felt very concerned for her. We would be walking down the street and she would suddenly shout 'Sorry' or 'Thank you'. When we went to the rugby club with her friends she would do it there too. She would jerk her head upwards and snap at the sun as if trying to eat it which was very embarrassing for her when people laughed and she couldn't concentrate on the game.

It is hard to try to communicate with Sophie about her feelings as I am not experiencing them with her and have no idea what it feels like. I try to ask her about it and when I get really annoyed and snap at her she simply replies 'I can't help it' or 'what!'. This is really annoying because she doesn't even realise what she is doing.

It is not a problem that Sophie has TS, it is just something she does which she tries hard to control, so we cannot blame her for it. It is part of who she is now.

Charlotte, aged 7 (Australia)

What it is like living with a brother with Tourette Syndrome

It's really annoying! My brother always gets aggravated and wants to fight. He gets out of control. He has tics and he can't help it. My brother, Wayne, is a twin and is 9 years old and he has Tourette Syndrome. He always loses things and forgets to bring his things like work, hat, music, glasses, drink bottle, even his lunch, to school. He often leaves his homework behind and he never wants to do it. My brother starts reading and Mum and Dad ask him to do something like brushing his teeth, but he says he cannot, 'I've got to finish the chapter!' And sometimes he gets very angry with people and hurts them.

Also Wayne has ADHD which is funny because he can concentrate on a book but he can't concentrate on other things. Sometimes it is worrying, because my brother often gets lost. We went skiing last holidays and Mum warned the instructor about his problems, but he got lost four times in one day! One time we were up the top of the mountain and Wayne skied ahead – he always wants to be out in front – and did not stop. Our instructor thought he was behind and they had lots of people looking for him. They found him 20 minutes later at the bottom of the mountain. Wayne thought he was behind the group and so he just kept going, but he went down a difficult blue run which we were not supposed to do. He also got lost on a big bike ride that we did and it was scary because it was beginning to get dark and we had to call the police out to help us find him.

My brother is really annoying, but I still love him!

Erica, aged 14 (UK)

My brother has Tourette Syndrome

My name is Erica, and I have a brother who suffers with Tourette Syndrome. He was diagnosed with TS in 2002 when he was around 12 years of age and he is now 14. His name is Buster.

His TS does not affect my life immensely but it does in a way I find quite irritating.

He spits (sometimes on people), chews paper or anything he can get his hands on and chucks it behind the television cupboards and sofas. He also gets nervous twitches such as blinking hard, flicking his arms and nodding his head, etc. Buster can get very aggressive and start hitting and punching and pinning people to the floor and spits on them or hurts them. He doesn't even know when to stop. If he gets silly or hyper, that's it! He would be hyper for ages.

He locks me out of the house and in some cases for quite a long period of time.

On some occasions he has left scars on my body because of hurting me. In any situation no matter where he is if he finds an opportunity to annoy someone he will take it – no hesitation.

Buster is very forgetful. He does something, forgets about it and goes on to the next thing. Once he forgot to turn off the grill, but luckily Mum smelt burning and ran downstairs to find the grill on.

He also forgets to take things to school. Buster really has no common sense. I don't know whether being forgetful is a result of TS but he certainly is forgetful.

When he was younger and hadn't been diagnosed with Tourette Syndrome he got bullied, but it was soon sorted out. He has been known to panic and do stupid things in important situations, resulting in bad things happening.

Even though he's a right pain in the bum he is my brother and I understand his condition and support him all the way. I love my brother.

Edda, aged 13 (Iceland)

I'm from Iceland. I'm a 13-year-old girl and have a brother who has Tourette Syndrome. My brother can be very entertaining, but when he is angry, he goes into a big blow-up. He screams. But it has lessened a lot, it was more when he was younger, but he is 8 years old now. When he was younger he screamed at least once a day or more, but it is rather seldom he shouts now.

What I find most inconvenient about him having TS is that he messes the home a lot. For instance he may be cleaning up his room and making it tidy and the next day it is in a mess again. And when he is eating, a lot goes onto the floor and he almost always gets very dirty around his mouth.

But sometimes it is just funny.

But not always because I myself have obsessive compulsive behaviour and because of that I want to have everything very tidy. I get very angry when things are messed up for me, so it can be very difficult for both of us to live under one roof. Because my brother is just my opposite and I'm his opposite. My brother is also almost always fixed into repeating his movements and he is also always wriggling. It was always very annoying but I am getting used to it now. But I find it unpleasant sitting by his side on a sofa when I am watching TV because he then wriggles a lot and cannot control it.

Angela, aged 12 (Italy)

A prayer

Dear God, please help my brother.
He is not very sick, so for you, it will be easy.
He has only tics, screams a little and uses swear words.
I am very unhappy to see him like this and I try to encourage
    him and give him lots of small kisses.
Also I tell him to be patient and that very soon all will be well.
By doing this, I make him smile and he strokes my hair.

Sarah, aged 17 (UK)

Living with a sibling who has Tourette Syndrome

February 2003 will be a time that I will remember forever, because that was the year my brother was diagnosed with Tourette Syndrome. Not only was it a worrying time, but a time when I felt relieved. This was because when he was 7 years old he developed a severe jolt within his body which we later learnt was a tic and his mood would change suddenly. We soon learnt that this would put a strain on members of our family, including me.

Back then, Tourette Syndrome was not well recognised and I found that when people heard of the term they would laugh and say that this illness was where they scream swear words. This used to wind me up as I believe that the real problem isn't the actual illness but the fact that people will be nasty because they don't understand about the syndrome. This later led me to be worried every time I brought a friend home in case they didn't understand or didn't come round again! But having this condition wasn't anything to be ashamed of and certainly shouldn't cause a problem to anyone else, and thankfully it didn't and people soon started to get used to hearing him deal with his problem and accepted it, just like I have.

As many may agree who are in the same situation as me, when a sibling has a certain condition, you become so well educated in that department that when they show the symptoms you become used to them, whereas people that are uneducated in the subject will not. As I have got older I have noticed that the illness is becoming more recognised and was surprised when whilst in a sixth-form assembly, they had organised a whole presentation on the disorder. Many people came up to me afterwards, saying that they didn't realise that Tourette Syndrome has so many symptoms attached to it, and that they felt they were more informed.

Tourette Syndrome is mainly a physical disorder, the symptoms including regular tics and shouting out random words or noises. However, I have noticed that it does affect you mentally as you reach the teenage years, when it hits its peak, and this is the side that does affect the sibling or relative more, in my opinion. Forever-changing mood swings and a low self-confidence are the two main things I have seen change my brother in recent years. This makes the environment at home sometimes difficult as suddenly my brother will have a mood swing over something that aggravates him, whether big or small.

Hearing Robert get very angry upsets not only me but also the others in the household, and however much I try to ignore it, I can't and this always causes us to fall out. I know that he can't help it and when I do get angry I try my hardest to think that the reason he does it is because of his frustration related to the illness.

Sometimes I think to myself I really feel for Robert because it really must be hard trying to control these tics in front of his friends, especially as three years ago he moved to a completely different school and the need to control them was even greater. When I have asked him in the past whether his friends have accepted that he has got TS and still continue being his friend or whether the opposite has happened, he always replies saying they have accepted it. I don't know whether to believe this or not, but having seen his mates come round and seeing how loud and sociable he is in front of them, I am pleased that people can see him for the person he is and not the condition he has.

Over the last couple of years his TS has tended to fluctuate sometimes, from being really powerful to not being there at all. But his tics have definitely got worse. I know it is awful for me to think this, but sometimes I have to look away because I cannot bear to see some of the things he can't help but do to his body such as hitting his knuckles together or punching his legs. But not once have I heard him complain about this and this makes me very proud of him and how strong a person he is, 'cause I know if that was me I would kick up a big fuss about it!!

Tourette Syndrome is one of a thousand disorders that are around and many other siblings may agree that with any syndrome the problem doesn't lay within the person who has the disorder, it is with people who surround the sufferer and don't consider them the social 'norm'.

ADULTS WITH TOURETTE SYNDROME

Tsui, aged 25 (Taiwan)

Nee Hao Ma? ('How are you?' in Mandarin)

I've had tics for nearly 20 years. I knew that it was called Tourette Syndrome five years ago. When I was studying in the schools, many kids of my age were not friendly with my tics. Since I'm tall for a Taiwanese, they did not do bad things physically to me, but hurt my heart often with their looks and attitudes. I guess that is the reason why I have few pals. Fortunately my family are all very tolerable and sweet to me. I have a soft mind to forgive others. Having graduated from the college, I was very lucky to get the job I'm busy with now. I told my boss about my TS on the first day I met him. He is so kind to accept me. Of course I work very hard for more than 12 hours per day too.

At the weekends, I go outdoors with youngsters of my kind for energy-consuming activity, such as basketball playing, swimming, rock climbing, etc. We believe that TS makes us energetic as super-kids or the incredibles. You see, Taiwan is an area with many earthquakes. We think that tics are just like earthquakes of us, in some aspects. After energy consumption of good things, there is less energy left for tics. Try it for a longer period. Never hope that one day of exercise will cure your tics. Keep doing it, there may even be some exacerbation initially, but you'll find out that it's true and you become much healthier after a period of regular exercise. We think that TS makes our brain energetic, and our body outside the brain must be active to get a real balance. Lazy TS kids will never get rid of their tics. We are a group of productive guys in society, not the lazy ones without TS.

Frances, aged 47 (UK)

There already

I have Tourette Syndrome. I am 47 years old and found out about five years ago. I'll explain. My son had funny movements and 'twitches' from the age of 4-and-a-half years old. He started with rocking when sitting very close to the TV when he got home from nursery. I told him to sit still and he said he was. As it was doing no harm I put it down to having just started school and I ignored it, although I found it a bit strange and kept an eye on him for any other strange behaviour.

After about two weeks, he started violently shaking his head. This lasted for several months, and whenever he was asked to stop, he replied either that he wasn't doing it or that he couldn't stop. His unusual movements changed regularly, with the next one taking over from the previous one. Eye rolling, arm shooting out to the side or up into the air, shoulder shrugging, facial grimaces, a funny walk (as if his foot kept getting stuck to the ground) etc. He also was constantly sniffing and being told to blow his nose.

At the age of about 6, he started a very loud throat-clearing noise. It occurred every waking moment and with every breath. His teacher called me into school, and whilst apologising profusely, said I had to take him to a doctor as he was disturbing the whole class and the classes on either side. A friend (who was a nurse with a husband who was a paediatrician) recommended that I get him referred to Dr X at my local hospital. My General Practitioner referred him straight away and we got an appointment quickly. Dr X said he had 'tics' and because they were so bad he prescribed haloperidol. Within three days I had a 'normal' son.

However, as the summer holidays came to a close, the tics started coming back, but not the awful noise he had earlier in the year.

One of the worst parts of my son's 'disorder' was the rage attacks. He would throw himself through the door when he got in from school, throw his bag in one direction and his coat in the other and start screaming and shouting if he could not have his own way immediately. The only way I could deal with this was to send him to a safe place, his bedroom, where he would slam the door so hard it almost came off its hinges, and he would proceed to 'trash' his room. He would stamp and throw things about, screaming and shouting. Then, after 20 to 30 minutes, he would come downstairs as if nothing had happened, say 'sorry' and ask for a drink. Occasionally he would have a 'rage' when we were out, and that was more difficult to cope with. I would usually just walk away from him (whilst checking he could come to no harm) and he would eventually follow and calm down.

We saw Dr X every six months. He was brilliant and even visited my son's school to advise the teachers how to cope with him (his behaviour was quite bad and I felt he had

ADHD although the doctor would not confirm this). I was given an article from a special needs magazine by the school's Special Educational Needs Coordinator (SENCO). It was about Tourette Syndrome, and it could have been written about my son. The penny dropped, and I realised my son probably had TS. I rang the Tourette Syndrome Association (TSA) and spoke to a very nice man, and when I described my son's behaviour he said it might well be TS and I needed to have him referred to a specialist. It took me over a year to get the doctor to diagnose my son with TS, although he had been absolutely brilliant throughout and treated him as if he did have TS, and then to get him referred to a specialist.

After another six month or so wait (we managed to be seen at an 'extra' clinic) we had an appointment with Professor Mary Robertson at the National Hospital for Neurology and Neurosurgery in London. Prof Robertson sent reams of questionnaires to us to complete and take to the appointment with us. She also wanted the whole family to attend so my son, husband, daughter and I went to the National. Prof Robertson asked many more questions, including 'Does anyone else in the family have Tourette Syndrome?'

I answered 'No' and she replied, 'But you have TS. I noticed at least three tics within the first ten minutes of the appointment, and I will have a consultation with your daughter, too.' My son was diagnosed with moderate Tourette Syndrome, ADHD and mild OCD. My daughter was later diagnosed with mild Tourette Syndrome and ADD (without hyperactivity), and although I was not officially diagnosed, it really made me think back to my childhood and I realised I probably did have mild TS and also mild OCD.

When I was a toddler I constantly washed my hands. As soon as I had the slightest bit of dirt on them I felt uncomfortable and had to wash them. I remember that I had a lot of infections and my mum was constantly taking me to the doctor's. There was a nurse there, and I can still remember the nightmares she gave me when she said to my mum 'If she [me] keeps on getting infections, she will have to go to boarding school to toughen her up' and the doctor telling my mum to 'let her play in the gutter, get dirty and get some immunity'.

I still don't like the feel of dirty hands but am usually able to fight the urge to constantly wash or am able to avoid situations where I will feel 'dirty', i.e. touching animals at a farm with the children. I was also obsessed with a tiny hole in the path of our front garden and would crouch down for ages wriggling my finger in the hole. I could not pass it by without doing this. However, I can't remember ever feeling that something bad would happen if I didn't do it.

When I was about 10 I had quite a bad tic – I was constantly opening my mouth as wide as I could. I would feel almost an itch in the corners of my mouth and the only way I could get rid of it was to stretch my mouth. My parents were constantly telling me to stop doing it, but I couldn't.

When I mentioned that I probably had mild TS to a friend I used to go to school with, she said, 'I always wondered why you were always wrinkling your nose. I assumed it was because your glasses were slipping down', although I can remember 'wrinkling my nose' even when I did not have my glasses on!

I also feel the urge to copy tics if they are suggested; if someone with TS is chatting on the phone to me and are explaining their or their child's symptoms, I have to 'do' their tics, either very discreetly or in my mind. The urge to copy is very strong if I see someone else ticcing.

Most of my friends and workmates have no idea I have TS, they just accept me as I am. It never stopped me from doing anything, and I took my 'O' levels along with the rest of my classmates. I have had several jobs, from secretarial to shelf stacking (which fitted in around the children and my husband's work), from bar work to working in an optician's.

I have always worked, and found that I need to work. It gives me space to be myself and not just a mum. It has not been easy bringing up two children with TS and associated disorders and it is *very* difficult to tell when the behaviour is due to them being naughty or to the TS/ADHD. I always tried to have boundaries, although they were probably more relaxed than for children without 'problems'.

As they have grown up, life has got easier. My son is fairly stable now on medication and the 'rages' are few and far between. He is currently studying for nine GCSEs – when he first started secondary school I did not expect him to do any, I thought he would have to do a vocational course!

If I could, I would wave a magic wand and cure TS. Unfortunately, there is no cure at the present time, although it can be managed with the right medication. I would not change my children for the world. They both have a brilliant sense of humour, which has helped us through the bad times. TS is a part of us and made us who we are.

Yossy, aged 37 (Japan)

Sah, Tobitatoh!! – Take off!!

Tourette made me make up my mind to hurt myself at that time in my young days. Tourette made me make up my mind to encourage everyone at present. Because of Tourette, I could not have a happy life. My dream was to be a pilot. So, I needed to pass the entrance exam at university. But Tourette made me shout, twitch and jump. Of course I could not only not attend a class, but also not take an exam in the silent room. In the end, I could not help dropping out of university. After dropping out, I became engaged in various jobs. I met various people. I was met with various experiences. It was hardship, mildness, kindness, anger, joy, despair, hope, sadness, and happiness. Everybody I had met with encouraged me and gave me precious memories. Because I had been given Tourette, I have been like this now. Thanks to Tourette, I can have an exciting life now. It has taken so many years to change my mind for the better against Tourette. The final decision made me happy for being Tourette. Now Tourette is part of my body. Thank you.

Lester, aged 31 (UK)

The odd boy in the class

Everyone must remember having someone a bit strange in their class at school. All must think, 'I'm glad I am not that person.' Well this is the story of being that odd boy in the class, of being the person that everybody looks at and thinks, 'Thank God I'm not like that.' This is my story. This is the story of a boy with Tourette Syndrome.

I started to tic when I was 5 years old. I began making bizarre funny noises, nothing like normal speech at all (which I could already use). There was no reason for them. They just came. I don't remember much of this time, but I learned afterwards that the noises I made had quite an effect on my parents, causing worry, concern and sometimes frustration. Once my mother had actually called my father back from work (it was the 1970s!) because I was driving her mad!

Then the noises went away, just as strangely as they had come. Several years later I began to twitch my head in a sideways movement, a bit like shaking it to say 'no', only more abrupt and strong. Time had moved on. I was now about 8 or maybe 9 years old, and singing in the choir at school. The problem was I looked out of place when singing with the choir on stage. The choirmaster simply didn't understand that I couldn't simply stop my movements and twitches. Everyone wanted to know why I couldn't just stop them. 'He must be nervous,' they all said. 'It must be a nervous tic.' At one stage tranquillisers were even suggested. Again I don't really remember what happened next. The problem just went away.

When I was 13, I went away to a big country boarding school. For the first time in five years I was at school with girls, and for the first time ever that began to matter to me. With the increase in self consciousness or awareness that growing up or adolescence brings, sadly came more tics. Now I had twitching of the head, this time several different types. I really knew what it meant to be alone, to be outcast, shunned and excluded by the children in my class. I was so odd and peculiar that almost no-one seemed to want to have anything to do with me, at least some of the time. Now I was 100 miles from my family with no-one to defend me.

At least when the lights went out I could twitch my head to my heart's content, happy in my own personal and private world. This did not last into my second year at the school. Having already been known as a misfit, I now began to make weird gulping noises too. From these there was no hiding away or escaping. In class or in the dormitory at night, there was no escape. Everybody knew. The worst moment of all came during a school play. I desperately wanted not to make any noise at all, but the harder I tried, the more I failed. During the quieter moments the whole auditorium in the theatre must have been able to hear the very loud gulping sounds I was making. People in the row behind leaned forward to ask the people sitting next to me, not me (!), why I was making the noises…like it was possible for anyone else to explain. I didn't even really know myself, all I knew was that I couldn't stop. I wanted the earth to swallow me up. I wanted to disappear.

Time went by. In spite of my early sensation of being so alone at boarding school I did form lasting friendships like other normal teenagers. There were even people who were less popular than me which was surprising to me. Funny, I looked at them and thought how glad I was not to be like that! My parents, sister and I attended family counselling for a while and I saw a child psychiatrist once at the age of 15 who mentioned a diagnosis. I only vaguely remember this, it may have been Tourette Syndrome, but it was very much downplayed.

By the age of 18 I had passed several exams and got good grades. My tics were improving by now. The noises had stopped a few years earlier and now I was passing for normal a lot of the time. I think most people I spent any amount of time with knew that I had tics, but that wasn't such a big issue any more. The company I kept was now older and less interested in my oddities or strangeness. I had moved towards a group of friends that were, like me, a bit eccentric or different. I got a temporary job working in an operating department after leaving school and through this I took the decision to go to medical school.

After a gap year and some interesting travels I started at medical school in central London in October 1993. It took a little while to completely shake off the sensation of being a misfit that I had picked up at boarding school, and I think I was still regarded as a little odd. I was more relaxed with this by then, though, and it didn't bother me so much. University presented a far wider range of society than I had experienced at boarding school and I met a lot of people that I liked and who liked me. Several years in I realised I was actually popular, at least in some circles. I had several interesting girlfriends. I took up rock climbing and became very involved with this both at university and beyond, meeting an even more diverse group of people. Finally I felt at ease.

I first took a BSc course and got a first class degree in 1996. I took time out of the medical course to do a PhD, furthering my reputation as an eccentric academic in which I had by now come to delight. I passed my PhD just before I turned 28. I was ten years out of school, confident, well-qualified and enjoying life. The challenge of my medical final degrees exams loomed before me.

About that time I was engaged in the psychiatry component of the undergraduate medical course. By now of course I knew a little bit about Tourette Syndrome and had realised that this might have been mentioned by the psychiatrist I saw 13 years before. I was relaxed enough with myself to have conversations with my classmates about whether or not I did have this syndrome, but we had come to no conclusion. During my psychiatry attachment I attended a lecture by Prof Mary Robertson, an expert on the syndrome. I listened hard to her describe the features of the syndrome and the experience of those who are affected by it. I will remember forever a slide showing the diagnostic criteria for Tourette Syndrome and the realisation that she was talking about me. Not me personally, but she was describing with great accuracy the phenomenon of my tics. Every last detail was correct. It gets worse when you want to stop. It gets worse when you talk about it. It gets better with alcohol. It gets better as you grow older. It was very clear that I had Tourette Syndrome.

I went to talk to Prof Robertson after her lecture. The conversation went something like this:

> Myself: 'I think I might have this syndrome…'

> Prof Robertson: 'Yes, I know.'

She had made the diagnosis purely from observing me during her lecture, something I later learned was not that uncommon for her. (Obviously I do still tic, but not as much as when I was a child.)

On the one hand I could not be that affected by Tourette Syndrome; I was at university, with lots of friends, interests, a girlfriend and all the usual things that go with someone in their late 20s. On the other hand tics had greatly shaped my earlier life. I learned many interesting facts from Prof Robertson. There were at that time about 3000 children being seen in Tourette Syndrome clinics in the UK. If, on the other hand, one were to do a survey of schoolchildren and look for those who fitted the criteria for a diagnosis (the features displayed on the slide that had triggered such recognition for me), one finds that about one in 100 children could be diagnosed with the syndrome. That makes nearly 100,000 children in the UK, meaning that there are over 90,000 children with tics out there who have not been diagnosed. I had found my place. I was one of those children.

I passed medical finals with several distinctions and went off to work as a junior doctor initially in Truro, Cornwall, then later in Inverness and Nottingham. I enjoy success now in all sorts of ways; with women, with work, with friends, with learning and professional exams, just as others do. I have recently acceded to membership of the Royal College of Physicians, involving three tough postgraduate exams. I have completed the first part of my training and I am soon to begin the next phase of my training in my chosen area of specialisation, infectious diseases medicine. I have lectured at university, and I hope to become an academic, that is a doctor who not only sees patients, but also does research, teaches, and writes books and medical papers. I am in a successful relationship and I am still rock climbing as a hobby. In short, I have come from being the odd boy in the class to leading a completely normal and very happy life.

People come in all sorts of shapes and sizes. Some are beautiful, others ugly. Some short, some tall, some oddly shaped. Some are generous, others selfish. Some are angry, some are too passive. Others still are balanced in these areas, but may have different faults. We all have different strengths and weaknesses. People have to accept you as you are, tics and all. They have their issues too, after all. But you must help them to accept you. You must accept yourself first. I have.

Prof Robertson adds: 'He now has the degrees BSc, MBBS, PhD – all by the age of 31 years. I know very few doctors who have been as successful as this – and I know a lot of doctors!'

Chapter 7

What can I do for my brother or sister with Tourette Syndrome?

There are many things you can do for your brother or sister with TS. These include learning about TS, supporting him or her or just being a caring person.

Why should I learn about TS?

In our experience, many young people talk about having mixed emotions about their siblings' TS. They feel angry, scared, sad and frustrated. However, a lot of this is due to simply not understanding the condition and feeling a bit scared. We are often frightened of things that we do not fully understand. One of the many useful things that you can do for your brother or sister is to read up on TS or at least ask your parents and the doctors about it. The more you know about TS, the less scary and the better informed you will be so that you will understand your brother or sister and help them.

Perhaps the most important thing you can do is to talk to your sibling. Ask him or her if they are OK. Occasionally you could ask him or her what it feels like to have TS or if there is anything that you can do to help him or her.

You may even want to come to your brother's or sister's appointment at the clinic, as I am sure you will be wondering what goes on there. Hopefully you will see that it is not as scary as you imagine and that the doctors are not that bad (most of us are friendly!). You will also be helpful to the doctors by telling them a little bit about your sibling. After all, you see him or her more than anyone else and are the best person to give an account of the problems.

Educate and teach others

Once you start to learn about TS then you will see that it is not as difficult to understand or as scary as you thought it was. You will find out that many people know very little about TS (including some doctors!). You will quickly also become an expert on TS! What a great position to be in. You will therefore be able to explain to other people about TS. This may be in school or at friends' houses. You may be out in public and someone may make a comment about your brother or sister or even give a disapproving look. If you feel confident, then you can explain that it is not his or her fault and that he or she cannot help making noises or twitching.

In our experience some brothers and sisters have written essays and projects on TS or spoken about TS in school assembly or lessons. This is helpful as it is likely that there are other children in your school with TS and they will benefit from others being educated.

Look after yourself

While you are getting on and being a good sibling, it is really important that you look after yourself. You have needs as well and sometimes you may feel that you are not getting enough attention from Mum and Dad. Talk to your parents about this. Also remember to do things for yourself and have treats. You are special too, and in order to help your brother or sister, you have to be in good health and be content. If you are irritable, tired or moody then you will not be able to help your sibling and that's when arguments start and resentment begins. So the most important thing we can say to you is *look after yourself*.

What can I do for my brother or sister?

Accepting your sibling for who he or she is is important. Look beyond the tics. See the positive aspects. Like the fact that you can laugh with him or her, see their strengths. Everyone is good at something, and your sibling will be special at something, too. This may be football, playing on the game boy or simply making people laugh.

Encourage his or her strengths and tell them how much you appreciate them. We are sure there are some things that he or she does for you. This may be helping you with homework, helping you with computer games or even supporting you when Mum and Dad are getting at you!

Occasionally you may want to surprise him or her by buying a gift or a small present – not just at Christmas or for a birthday.

The best thing you can do is to be supportive.

So what do I get out of it?

It is difficult growing up with a sibling who is different. Many young people have brothers or sisters with special needs or medical problems. A lot of young people in this situation have grown up and written about their experiences. They all say they have become a better person because of their sibling's differences. You will understand difference in individuals and become more tolerant of other people's difficulties. You will be able to help your friends more and have a better understanding of other people's difficulties. People will warm to you because of your personality and understanding. We tend to want to be with people who are kind and understanding. You will also appreciate the simple things in life and hopefully be a more contented person. Of course later on in life, your brother and sister will come to appreciate you and you will have a special loving relationship, which is unique. Your family ties will also be stronger.

Positive aspects of being a sibling of someone with TS
A sibling of someone with TS will:

- develop increased tolerance of differences
- become more understanding of other people
- find that other people will want to be your friend because you are caring
- develop skills for coping with life's problems
- contribute to society by helping others
- become a special advocate for your brother or sister
- appreciate simple things in life, like good health.

The Mock Turtle's song

'Will you walk a little faster?' said the whiting to a snail.
'There's a Touretter close behind us, and he's treading on my tail.'
See how what he wants to say can come out in advance.
What should you do for him? Let him join the dance!

There are lots of things that you can do,
Smile, be nice and give hugs too,
Give him a present or toy now and then,
Don't be cross, shout or 'Get even!'

He feels it's not fair that he makes a noise,
So, sometimes he can't play with other boys,
So give him a cuddle and make him feel good,
And treat him with care, as we all should.

Mary M. Robertson
With apologies to Lewis Carroll

Chapter 8

What is the future for a young person with Tourette Syndrome?

Will a young person with TS always have TS?

We don't know for certain what is going to happen to any of us. In many ways we cannot say what the outcome will be for young people with TS. What we can say, however, is that the majority of people with TS will have symptoms that reach a

peak at about 10 to 12 years of age. This can cause a lot of problems for the individual as it is usually at this age that we start to be more self-conscious and pay more attention to peer groups and social relationships. It is also at this age that we start to take an interest in boyfriends and girlfriends, so all-in-all this is a really tricky time.

The good news is that by the age of 18, many people will have lost a lot of their tics or at least have tics which are less troublesome. In addition, many of the difficulties associated with tics also lessen, such as some of the ADHD symptoms.

A number of children with TS will go on to have TS symptoms in adult life. As mentioned in Chapter 1, for some the TS becomes part of them – really like a sort of friend. If the adult needs help then there are also services and special clinics that may help with TS. In fact most of the research done on TS is done on adult patients.

Will a young person with TS lead a 'normal' life?

There is no reason why a young person with TS should not lead a normal life. Yes, he or she will get a job, do exams, have a boyfriend/girlfriend, get married, have children, play football, go dancing, etc. In other words, they will do the same as everybody else. Many young people with TS have grown up to achieve their goals and potentials. There are some people who have gone on to excel in their chosen fields (see below).

Have any famous people had Tourette Syndrome?

There are a number of outstanding people who have had symptoms of TS who have gone on to be outstanding academics, musicians or leading sportsmen and women in their field. Here are three such people who have been an inspiration to others.

Dr Samuel Johnson

Dr Samuel Johnson was born in 1709 in Staffordshire, England. He was a very wise and intelligent man who wrote many essays and poems. He is mostly famous for publishing the first-ever English dictionary in 1755. He is reported to have had many motor tics and vocal tics. The vocal tics included whistling and echolalia. He also had the habit of uttering bits of the Lord's Prayer into his normal conversation. Samuel Johnson died in 1784 and is buried in Westminster Abbey.

Jim Eisenreich

Jim Eisenreich is a famous American baseball player. He has TS and has talked about it at numerous meetings in America. His first symptoms were rapid eye-blinking and hyperactivity. He was not diagnosed with TS until 17 years later. He has played for the Minnesota Twins, Kansas City Royals, Philadelphia Phillies and the Los Angeles Dodgers.

Tim Howard

Tim Howard is one of the best-known goalkeepers in the world. He currently plays for Manchester United, having previously played for the New York/New Jersey Metrostars. He has also played in goal for the USA national team. He was a member of the USA Olympic Team in the Sydney Olympics in 2000. He has won numerous awards for his football skills as well as awards for his charity work on Tourette Syndrome.

Looking forward – for my brother and sister

I have a sweet but naughty little sister,
And a little brother – just two years old,
And to all of us who dearly love her
And him – they're really worth their weight in gold.

When they, despite TS, are grown to man's estate
They shall be so very proud, and also very great
And tell doctors and the other girls and boys
Not to meddle with my very own special toys.

TS will not hinder them when they do grow up,
And hopefully champagne will always fill their cup.
They can be happy, marry and find a good job,
They can be successful, and never again will sob.

They will find a Treasure Island, where all kids will be well
And all will play together, and for none it will be hell,
Some can be really famous, and save a lot of goals
For all the rest – just be happy and contented souls.

Mary M. Robertson
With apologies to both Robert Louis Stevenson
and an unknown author

The original versions of these poems were written by the famous poets whom we have acknowledged and thanked. We thought it would be fun to combine our love of TS and poetry.

Useful resources

Tourette Syndrome (UK) Association
P.O. Box 26149
Dunfermline, KY12 7YU
www.tsa.org.uk

Tourette Syndrome (USA) Association
42–40 Bell Boulevard
Bayside, NY 11631-2820
www.tsa-usa.mgh.harvard.edu

Tourette Syndrome (Japan) Association
4–24–10–406 Hon-Cho
Kokubunji, Tokyo 185-0012
Japan

Icelandic Tourette Association
Hatun 10b, 9. haeo
101 Reykjavik
Iceland

Tourette Syndrome Association of Australia
P.O. Box 1173
Maroubra, NSW 2035
Australia

Tourette Scotland
Support Base
17b Hospital Street
Perth PH2 8HN
www.tourettescotland.org

ADD Information Services (UK)
P.O. Box 340
Edgware, Middx HA8 9HL
www.addiss.co.uk

OCD Action (UK)
22–24 Highbury Grove
London N5 2EA
www.ocdaction.org.uk

OCD-UK
P.O. Box 8115
Nottingham N67 1YT
www.ocduk.org

'Youngsters with Tourette Syndrome will find comfort and good humour in this superbly written book by Professor Mary Robertson and Dr Uttom Chowdhury, recognized experts in the treatment and scientific research of Tourette Syndrome. Their compassion and deep understanding of their patients and their families are unparalleled.'

– *Judit Ungar, President and Sue Levi-Pearl, VP,*
Medical and Scientific Program, Tourette Syndrome (USA) Association

'I am delighted to recommend this book, which is devoted to helping young people understand TS. It is not only written by two highly experienced doctors but also includes an interesting collection of personal experiences of people affected by the syndrome. Young people more than anyone may feel they are alone in facing the challenges of life and this book is a very valuable source of support and information for all families affected by TS.'

– *Jeremy Stern, Chair of Tourette Syndrome (UK) Association*

Do you have Tourette Syndrome, TS for short, or does someone in your family? If so, then you will have noticed that sometimes they do or say things when they do not mean to. These tics, as they are called, can be embarrassing. It's all right, though: lots of people either have TS or love somebody with TS. You are not alone.

Why Do You Do That? is an age-appropriate source of information on Tourette Syndrome for children and adolescents aged 8 to 16. Uttom Chowdhury and Mary Robertson describe and explain tics and TS in clear, child-friendly terms and offer practical tips on how to live with and support someone with TS. This accessible book is an invaluable guide for families affected by TS, particularly for siblings of children with TS.

Uttom Chowdhury is a Consultant in Child and Adolescent Psychiatry for Bedfordshire and Luton Mental Health and Social Care Partnership Trust and an Honorary Consultant for the Social Communication Disorders Clinic at Great Ormond Street Hospital, London. His clinical and research interests include Tourette Syndrome, Obsessive Compulsive Disorders and Autistic Spectrum Disorders. **Mary Robertson** is Emeritus Professor of Neuropsychiatry at University College London and Honorary Consultant at St George's Hospital. She is an Honorary Medical Advisor to five Tourette Syndrome Associations. She has authored three and edited two books and has had over 240 medical publications and over 70 poems published.

Jessica Kingsley *Publishers*
116 Pentonville Road
London N1 9JB, UK

400 Market Street, Suite 400
Philadelphia, PA 19106, USA

www.jkp.com

cover design by C.P.Ranger

US $14.95

ISBN 1-84310-395-8

9 781843 103950